LOOK 10 YEARS
YOUNGER
FEEL 10 YEARS
BETTER

LOOK 10 YEARS YOUNGER
FEEL 10 YEARS BETTER

DR JAMES SCALA
& BARBARA JACQUES

PIATKUS

© 1991 James Scala and Barbara Jacques

First published in 1991 by
Judy Piatkus (Publishers) Limited
5 Windmill Street
London W1P 1HF

British Library Cataloguing in Publication Data
Scala, Dr James
Look 10 years younger, feel 10 years better.
I. Title   II. Jacques, Barbara
613.7

ISBN 0–7499–1056–9

Edited by Maggie Daykin
Line illustrations by Paul Saunders
Fashion illustrations on pages 72–77
by Caroline Bays
Design by Paul Saunders

Photo credits
Photograph of Joan Collins (1988) by Gary Bernstein. Photographs of Joan Collins
(1955 and 1988), Cher (1965) and Robert Redford (1967) copyright
© The Kobal Collection. Photograph of Cher (1987) copyright © Warner Bros Inc.,
and loaned by The Kobal Collection. Photograph of Robert Redford (1988) copyright
© Rex Features Ltd.

Other photographs by Ron Sutherland

Typeset by Phoenix Photosetting, Chatham, Kent
Printed and bound in Great Britain by
The Bath Press, Bath, Avon

To Nancy and Brian
You have proved a point that teaches: people can accomplish anything, if they don't care who gets the credit. Many thanks.

ACKNOWLEDGEMENTS

Our grateful thanks to all the following:

Nancy Scala and Brian Jacques, who through their unselfish love and dedication gave us just what we needed when the going got tough.

Al Zuckerman, who is a truly supportive person.

The staff at Harrods, too numerous to mention, for their wonderful help which went beyond the call of duty. But especially Brian Ames, Julia Eccles, Tak Lee and Ann Wilkinson for their help and support, especially when it came to helping out with the clothes from Jumo, Escada and Jobis.

Paul Newland, from Vidal Sassoon, who paved the way for Barbara to meet exciting colourist Annie Humphreys, and see the talents of Billi Currie, who created sheer magic with the models' hair (between pages 112 and 113). Billi works in the Vidal Sassoon salon at Whiteleys of Bayswater, 151 Queensway, London W2 (071–792 2741). For details of your nearest Vidal Sassoon salon, please telephone 071–409 1695.

Lori Fiori from Prescriptives Cosmetics, for her time, help and support. And John Gustafson whose artistry with colour cosmetics transformed our models (between pages 112 and 113). Also to Fiona Slattery for her help and support.

John Cullen from the Trusthouse Forte Hotel, Crick, Northamptonshire, for his enthusiasm for the book and his assistance in allowing Barbara to field test some of her ideas.

The models – Anne Shelmerdine, Sally Wood, Avis Charles, Susan Meers and Anne Ponsonby – for giving us their time and patience.

And at Piatkus, thanks to Judy Piatkus, Philip Cotterell and Gill Cormode for seeing the potential of the book and getting firmly behind it. Gill's help, advice and direction helped us considerably. Also Heather Rocklin, whose logical approach and quiet soothing voice were invaluable to us all in the latter stages, and who was largely responsible for putting the manuscript to bed. Also Maggie Daykin – we don't know how you did it, but you did!

Contents

Introduction

A youthful outlook

Is age creeping up on you? Have you noticed your first grey hair, or is your hair getting thinner, or even sparse? Have you a few crow's feet, the beginnings of a double chin or a little sagging here and there? Is it becoming more difficult to get rid of those extra pounds of weight? Do you pile things up at the bottom of the stairs until you have to go up, or pop out to the shops without lipstick or with laddered tights, hoping that no one will see you? Are you just too tired to bother?

If you are a man, have you stopped cleaning the car or your shoes as often as you used to? Do you see the unkempt designer stubble (scruffy look) fashion trend as a good idea because it means that you don't have to shave? Have you given up on sporting activities? Do you always drive or ride rather than walk any distance?

Changing for the better

Age does have a habit of creeping up on us, unnoticed at first. Then we catch sight of ourselves in a mirror or shop window one day and realise that we don't look as youthful as we did at 18, 28, or even 38 for that matter. Face up to it. Are you allowing your youthfulness to slip by too quickly due to poor nutrition (too much of the wrong food and too little of the right), too many bad habits and too few good ones?

Bad eating habits develop from the instant gratification that unhealthy food provides. Good eating habits develop when you recognise that personal health is a full-time responsibility we all have. These good habits will add years to your life and life to your years.

Fortunately, good habits take no longer to learn than bad ones. The time it takes to make the changes we suggest in this book is negligible in comparison to the extra hours you will enjoy each day – hours which were previously lost either falling asleep in front of the television or failing to get up early in the morning.

Throughout this book, whether we are writing about weight, body type, skin, hair, eyes or teeth, you will find that we first deal with the all-important health factors. No matter how adept you become at applying make-up, and skilled in choosing flattering clothes, it will just be a clever cover-up unless you also work on improving your body and general health. How can you look good if you don't feel good? You certainly can't for long!

Weight and body type

If your body shape or weight is a serious worry, then you can do something about it, starting now. In Chapter 3 we help you discover your figure image and explain that being over or under weight is not an insoluble problem. Our advice about nutrition (and sensible eating) and exercise in Chapters 2 and 4 will help you to regain and maintain a healthy weight, and re-shape your body as necessary for a better, more youthful physique and good looks.

Knowing one's body type – and learning how the line and design of clothes can make you look lighter or heavier, taller or shorter, younger or older – brings immediate, positive cosmetic results. Making the best of what you have may initially mean using a little camouflage here or there, or directing attention to parts of your body which can stand up to being scrutinised. So what! It will make you look and feel good straightaway and encourage you to work at improving your body for even better, longer-term results. In Chapter 5 we give advice on choosing the most appropriate and flattering clothes for your shape.

Our bodies are never static, and how well they serve us depends on whether we maintain and 'rebuild', or neglect and 'destroy' ourselves. Whatever your age, your body has already rebuilt itself over and over again, with the results that you now see in your mirror. If the reflection is not to your liking you *can* change it.

In Chapter 3 you will learn how to analyse your body fat and set a realistic weight-target for yourself. Once you understand your own body fat, you can develop a lifelong weight and exercise programme to regain and maintain youthful vigour.

Skin

Regardless of skin type, around the age of 30 for a woman and 40 for a man, skin can start to sag. Wrinkles, crow's feet and age spots may begin to appear, making our skin less smooth, our age and our general health easier to guess correctly. The skin on our neck and hands generally ages first, because it is thinner here than on the rest of the body (except for the immediate eye area). Exposure to sun, smoking, fierce central heating and poor diet all speed up this natural ageing process.

However, thanks to modern research and development, it has been discovered that you can hold back these ageing processes by what you begin to do *now*. You can also improve the general appearance of your skin.

In Chapter 7 you will learn about skin, your largest organ. Skin has no secrets and tells everyone how it is nourished. You will learn how to recognise your skin's nutritional needs and how to satisfy them. Your beauty will not only be skin deep, it will be a reflection of your total health – you will look and feel younger.

If you are a woman, well chosen and correctly used make-up will always enhance your natural appearance and make you look younger. However, if you are using outdated methods of application, old-fashioned products or ones that may be too 'heavy' in texture, you will be making yourself look older rather than younger. In Chapter 7 you will also find out all you need to know about choosing and using the most suitable colours for you.

Hair

Your hair is affected by the same factors as your skin, and can soon show signs of ageing and stress. Healthy hair begins deep down in the follicle where each hair grows. If you give your hair the correct nourishment, it will radiate health. Loss of hair, premature greying, or the wrong colour or hair style for your face shape can all add years to your looks. Hair that is healthy, a good colour, well cut and appropriately styled does just the opposite – and is a great morale booster. In Chapters 2 and 8 you will discover how you can improve your hair condition, style and colour.

Teeth

Does your smile let you down? Do you instinctively put your hand over your mouth when you smile? Are any of your teeth uneven or missing, badly stained or discoloured? Do your gums bleed or feel sensitive when you clean your teeth or eat certain foods? The main thing to realise is that you don't have to go through life with a hang-up about your teeth, nor is it inevitable that one day you will need dentures! There have been wonderful developments in dentistry and you can do something positive about having a lovely smile which shows healthy, even, sparking white teeth. See Chapter 10.

Healthy teeth and gums must be nurtured by daily care, which includes correct hygiene and nutrition. You will learn that a few good habits will keep your teeth and gums healthy for life and put a radiant smile on your face.

Eyes

No one needs telling how important eyes are or how precious sight is and we are all aware of the compelling attraction of clear, bright eyes. So let's not neglect them. We not only advise you how to keep them healthy, but how to choose flattering frames for your face shape if you wear glasses. See Chapter 9.

Hands, feet and nails

Apart from your neck and posture, nothing will show your age more than your hands, feet and nails. They quickly show signs of neglect, poor circulation and ageing, because they are at the end of the blood line, and sluggish circulation or poor health can leave hands and feet cold, rough looking and with nails that split, peel and break. In Chapters 2 and 4 we tell you how to improve your circulation through sensible nutrition and regular exercise. In Chapter 10 we give advice on caring for hands, feet and nails from the outside.

Nails are windows to your circulation. You will learn how to nourish them to keep them strong. By doing so, you will make your whole body healthy.

Good posture

Your posture and how you carry yourself reflect your inner feelings and can affect how people respond to you. The man or woman who is feeling old, ill, tired or inferior, or has given up on themselves in body and mind, will show all these things by the way they carry themselves. Someone who carries themself upright and tall gives an impression of youthfulness, optimism and soundness in health and spirit. In Chapter 11 we show you how to check and, if necessary, correct your posture.

Good posture isn't an accident: it's a commitment to excellence. It not only helps you look good on the outside, but helps you feel good from the inside – it optimises all your bodily functions.

Mental outlook

If you are experiencing apathy, fatigue or stress, your body is sending out warning signals that you should heed. Some 'tender loving care' can work wonders. So do take stock of 'you', your personal life and see what changes you could make to put things 'right'. Success begins with a vision. You must visualise what you will become and you will become what you visualise. What you once saw as excuses, you will now see as opportunities on which to build your future.

Men or women who are 30- or 40-plus, and who look and feel really good, have usually made a conscious decision to work positively in that direction. They have worked out the right fitness programme for them: they eat in moderation, take food supplements, exercise sufficiently, sleep well, and generally groom their bodies as a daily habit. You can learn how to do the same, by reading all of this book.

Facing up to facts

Before beginning this transformation, however, you need to carry out an honest assessment of your present state. In the comfort and privacy of your bedroom, remove your clothes (put on a swimsuit if you prefer not to face the naked truth), and take a good look at yourself in a full-length mirror. Bearing in mind all the aspects of body care we have mentioned, ask yourself which are the areas you most need to work on, and set yourself realistic goals. Once you have achieved them, you can move the goal posts a little and work for even better results, if necessary. Much is possible, we promise you. So let's begin.

Barbara Jacques
Jim Scala

CHAPTER ONE

Living Longer, Living Better

Look in a mirror. Do you realise that you're looking at the product of 18 billion years of evolution? That makes us special, and worthy of loving care. Learning how to give ourselves such care is what this book is all about.

Learning and loving are essential to a complete life. We start learning in the womb and don't stop until death. Human character isn't complete if we don't experience the giving and receiving of love. One condition for being able to love seems to be that love must begin with self. You must love yourself so you can give love to others and receive it from them.

Self-respect is essential to self-love. Again, you must show respect to get respect, and it begins with yourself. If you respect and value your body, you will be repaid many times with a longer, richer life; you will set an example for others.

Good health makes life more abundant. With health you can take advantage of all this world has to offer: enjoy more keenly the passon of involvement, feel the ecstasy of achievement, and the agony of defeat. Most important, you will experience the supreme emotion . . . Love!

Optimum health recognises that we're all different! You are unique right down to each of the 50 trillion cells that make your body. Striving for optimum health means making your body as healthy as possible. Only then will you reach your maximum potential, live better and longer.

AIM FOR A LONGER LIFE

Focus on a clear, single objective, then your short-term goals will fall into place. An excellent long-term objective is simple: optimise your health to live as long as possible. This means minimising things that detract from optimum health.

Whenever I talk about optimum health, someone says, 'Oh, but that means living a dull old life.' My reply is a firm NO – just the opposite. You will do, see, feel and achieve more because you'll be healthier. You will sleep more soundly, awake more quickly and smell the roses more keenly.

A baby born in 1990 could easily be alive to celebrate New Year's Eve in the year 2100. Just think of it. He or she can live that long based on what we know today about prevention of illnesses that shorten our lives – without taking into account the fantastic discoveries that will be made in health care over the next 110 years.

How to increase your life expectancy in the 1990s is clear. You've got to prevent cancer and heart disease, avoid high blood pressure and reduce degenerative diseases such as osteoporosis, arthritis, kidney disease and diabetes. Don't rely on transplant surgery to save you because the economics of it are impossible. Prevention's the thing! If you avoid these problems, or put them off as long as possible, you could add as much as 30% to your life-span. Most important, we know how to do this now.

The table below summarises life expectancy for people living in 1990. The middle column, 'How Much Longer You Will Live', represents a realistic average of how many more years you can expect to live. The next column shows 'How Much Longer You Can Live' – the years remaining with a possible 30% increase if you avoid heart disease and cancer.

Life expectancy Vs. potential in 1990

Age now	Years remaining 'How much longer you will live'	Potential 'How much longer you can live'
Birth	82	107
20	60	78
40	39	51
60	23	30
80	9	12

How do you do it? First, let's look at the risk factors. Then we will determine how old you are physiologically as compared to what the calendar tells you.

Risk factors: physiological age

Heart disease, more generally called cardiovascular disease (CVD for short) is the general clogging of the heart and other arteries; CVD and cancer are characterised by probabilities. If you're on the wrong side of these probabilities, your risk of contracting the diseases is high. In contrast, get on the right side and your risk is low. Many risk factors are common to both diseases, so lowering your risks of getting one of the diseases also reduces your risk of getting the other.

'Risk factor' is simply a way of expressing some factor that increases the chances of getting a specific illness. We are interested in risk factors that are diet and lifestyle related because we can do something about them. We will consider heredity, when appropriate, because it is also possible to reduce the risk that you may have inherited.

Risk factors common to cardiovascular disease and cancer

- Heredity – Who your parents are
- Being overfat – Are you carrying too much fat on your body?
- Not enough cereals, fruits and vegetables in your diet
- Chronic constipation from a lack of fibre
- Inadequate nutrient intake (not enough vitamins and minerals)
- Excessive alcohol consumption (over 3% of calories)
- Smoking or another chemical dependency, including medication
- Excessive stimulant consumption (a chemical dependency)
- Depression or a poor outlook (not enough optimism)
- Poor exercise habits (less than three times weekly)
- Lack of aerobic exercise

Risks specific to cardiovascular disease

- High blood pressure
- Elevated blood-cholesterol
- Excessive blood-fats
- Diabetes
- Emotional stress

Risks specific for cancer

- Living and working in a polluted area
- Excess high-risk foods, such as those containing a high proportion of fat, and processed meats
- Inadequate protective-nutrients and beneficial foods
- Having colds or flu more than once a year.

THE LONGEVITY TEST

The following test compares your physiological age with your chronological age, by looking at the age of your cardiovascular system. It is based on the saying, 'We are only as old as our arteries.' If your results show you are 'older' than your chronological age, don't despair – these findings can be reversed.

In taking this test you will need to know your weight, blood pressure and cholesterol count. Weight and blood pressure are easily self-determined by means of scales and electronic instruments designed to measure blood pressure; these devices are called sphygmomanometers and are available from chemists. Assessing your cholesterol requires the taking of a small blood sample which can then be 'read', so you will need to consult your doctor. If you want to improve your health and retain youthful vigour, do begin by getting this vital information.

Score the test by starting with your present age and either add or subtract years as each question indicates.

Anti-ageing factors

1. If blood pressure is 120/80 or less, subtract two years from your age.   −2

2. If you are under 40 and your cholesterol count is less than 4.7 (millimoles per litre of blood), subtract one year. If you are over 40, but less than 50, and it is below 5.2, subtract one year. If you are over 50 and it is less than 5.5, subtract one year.   −1

3. If you are in good physical condition and exercise regularly (moderately), subtract one year.   −1

4. If you have no chronic conditions (e.g. high blood pressure, arthritis), subtract two years.   −2

5. If you have no respiratory problems (e.g. asthma, emphysema), subtract one year.   −1

6. If your resting heart rate, when sitting, is less than 60 beats per minute, subtract one year.   −1

7. If you have good night vision (with or without spectacles), subtract one year.   −1

Ageing factors

1. If your blood pressure (uncorrected by medication) is over 135/95, add three years to your age.   +3

2. If you are more than 10% overweight, add 3 years.   +3

3. If your cholesterol is over 6.7 (millimoles per litre of blood), add two years.   +2

4. If you smoke, add three years.   +3

5. If you have more than two alcoholic drinks a day, add one year.   +1

6. If you don't recover to normal heart rate within 10 minutes after exercising vigorously, add one year.   +1

7. If you are anaemic, add one year   +1

8. If you have poor immunity, that is, if you become infected easily or catch colds and flu easily, add one year.   +1

9. If you suffer from constipation or use laxatives regularly, add two years.   +2

10. If you always seem to feel tired and are fatigued, add one year.   +1

11. If your resting pulse rate is more than 80 beats per minute when sitting, add one year   +1

12. If you have a poor short-term memory, add one year.   +1

13. If you have sexual difficulties (men erection; women lubrication), add one year.   +1

How to evaluate your score

The best score gives you a biological age that is less than your chronological age. For example, my biological age is nine years less than my chronological age. That means, from the standpoint of ageing, I have gained nine extra years.

Better still, look up life expectancy in a register of vital statistics; most general almanacs contain the same information. The chart lists your age with a tabulation showing years remaining. Let's use me as an example. My physiological age is my chronological age minus nine; that's 55 minus 9, yielding 46. The years remaining for a 46 year old are 29.3 versus 21.5 for a 55 year old. So, add 29.3 to 55 and it comes to 84.3 versus 76.5, or a 36% increase, all because I exercise, watch my diet and maintain a healthy lifestyle. But is it worth adopting a healthy lifestyle? It certainly is if you want to have a younger biological age, and it sure is working for me.

Let's review

Now you have taken the test, we'll review the questions, explaining what they mean and how you can start some positive programmes to get you on the right track.

Anti-ageing factors   These are a measure of how your vital signs stack up against the changes we all experience during the ageing process. These factors estimate the fitness of your cardiovascular system and the rate at which your arteries are becoming clogged up. They also estimate the fitness of your respiratory system.

Ageing factors   Ageing factors measure the speed of deterioration of your body. Is yours deteriorating faster or more slowly than that of most other people your age?

- The first three questions concern the major risk factors for heart disease, blood pressure, cholesterol and weight. Get all three down, and you will add years to your life and life to your years.

- Questions 4 and 5 should never add to anyone's years. If you have added years for these, your answer to question six has to be poor because a person who practises chemical abuse can't possibly have good exercise recovery. Stop these habits.

- Questions 7 and 8 give an index of how resilient you will be to assaults on your body. If you are anaemic, either your diet is poor or there is a more serious cause. Get it diagnosed and treated by a doctor.

- Question 9 indicates whether you're a candidate for intestinal problems, including cancer and diverticulosis. Your cholesterol would be lower if you had better, natural regularity. More importantly, you don't have good dietary habits.

- Questions 10 and 11 relate to fitness. Better fitness is better health. Chronic fatigue is generally caused by being overweight, having a poor diet and poor exercise habits – and often clinical depression. It can indicate excessive use of stimulants. If your resting pulse is 80 or more, you're probably unfit. If you are fit and it's over 80, a doctor should find out why.

- Questions 12 and 13 ask whether or not you're keeping active. The old saying, 'If you don't use it, you lose it', is correct for every organ in your body, especially your brain.

This test helps you estimate whether or not you are ageing at an average rate. Preferably, you're progressing at a slower than average rate and you have more years ahead than your age indicates.

But suppose you come out with a biological age above your chronological age. What do you do? Analyse the questions and understand why you're ageing more rapidly than necessary. Did you know that, by losing weight and confronting other dietary issues, you can lower your biological age in as little as six months?

Now you are ready to start a new, more positive and healthy life.

· CHAPTER TWO ·

Eat Smart, Live Longer

Your score in the Longevity Test given in the previous chapter can be dramatically improved by eating the right food and exercising regularly. Diet and exercise are synergistic, which means that the results of both diet and exercise together are more than you'd expect by simply adding one to the other.

Results of a good diet begin immediately, but build slowly. You will see a healthier complexion in the mirror in a few days, stronger nails in a couple of weeks and better hair in a little more than a month. You will sleep more soundly, wake up more easily, have more energy and your stamina will improve – you will feel as good at the end of the day as at the beginning. Within six months, you will have reversed the effects of years of overlooking your health. You will feel ten years younger.

People improve slowly and it is easy to forget how you were six months ago, so it is important to keep notes on your progress. Weigh yourself frequently. Take your pulse now and then. Recall how you used to sleep or how difficult it was to get up. Look in the mirror, notice your complexion, the sheen of your hair, and the strength of your fingernails. Take the Longevity Test again.

Now let's go and eat!

EATING FOR LIFE

We will start with general guidelines on how to choose the right food for main meals, snacks and social occasions. You need to think about food several days ahead, because some things apply weekly, others daily. Don't waste calories! Many people increase their guilt level from eating the wrong things. That will never happen if you make your calories count.

Use a small, spiral-bound notebook to keep an account of what, when, why and where you eat. I divide my pages into columns to make it easier. The 'why' and 'where' will help you get in touch with your food habits. Ask yourself, 'Why am I eating this?' Sometimes it is because of your surroundings or the people you are with. Once you get into this habit you will be able to set realistic food goals.

Review your food-scorecard after each day; write a few sentences on how you did and identify things you could do to improve your food choice.

Dietary rules and goals

Eating for a longer life must satisfy five daily rules:

1. Balance calories for your ideal weight: calorie input should equal calorie output; don't gain or lose weight.

2. Eat for low fat and high fibre. When in doubt, eat for bulk; think vegetarian!

3. Balance oils. Eat fish three times weekly. Always use olive oil when in doubt about the oil to use.

4. Nature's bulbs daily. Garlic, onion, shallots, and other bulbous roots daily as condiments.

5. Colour besides green. Every day be sure to get some deep-red vegetable or fruit. Deep-red vegetables and fruit contain pigments that help prevent cancer.

These rules, and the Longevity Diet set out on pages 24 and 25, will help guide you in your daily and weekly food selections. If you follow this eating plan faithfully, you'll meet three dietary goals:

1. Your calories would come from about 25% or less fat, 10 to 15% protein, and 50 to 65% carbohydrate. This balance is about as good as you can get.

2. You will get about 1 ounce (30 grams) of dietary fibre daily with the right balance. This puts you in the top 15% of people who don't get intestinal problems. You will avoid the most common problems of ageing and also greatly reduce your risk of several types of cancer.

3. Your oil balance will be fine. It'll have the correct balance of saturated and unsaturated oils with enough oils from the newly recognised group – the omega-3s.

LONGEVITY DIET

I call this plan the Longevity Diet because it is designed to help you live longer and live better. It is also easily adapted to weight loss or weight gain.

You might recognise this diet as a modified 'balanced-diet.' In many respects, it is a balanced diet, but it is adapted from dietary needs that prevent the degenerative diseases of ageing. If you follow this diet and use the basic supplement given at the end of this chapter, you will always enjoy optimum nutrition and health.

Fruits and Vegetables: 5 Servings Daily

1. Serving = Fruit: ½ cup cut-pieces or berries, ¼ melon or a piece of whole fruit such as an apple, orange, banana, etc.
Vegetables: 1 cup (3½ oz or 100 g) raw or about ½ cup cooked (or a medium carrot, for example). Two medium potatoes (or ½ cup cooked brown rice).

Your daily allowance should include:

- One serving daily of deep-green or dark-red vegetables

- One serving daily of both a fruit and vegetable must be eaten raw

- One serving of beans daily; three varieties each week

- One green salad daily, with some red colour

Grains and Cereals: 4 Servings Daily

1. Serving = ⅓ cup cereal; 1 slice whole-grain bread; 1 whole-grain roll; ½ cup cooked corn, wheat, oats, etc.

Your daily allowance should include:

- One serving of high-fibre natural cereal (three varieties weekly) with low-fat milk from your milk allowance (see below).

Natural Bulbs (Condiments): Unlimited Servings Daily

1. Serving = A generous portion to flavour food naturally.
Minimum: One serving daily; you can't get too much garlic, onions, shallots, etc.

Milk and Dairy Products: 3 Servings Daily

1. Serving = 8 fl oz (235 ml) low-fat milk, 6 fl oz (180 ml) low-fat yogurt or 1½ oz (40 g) low-fat cheese

Protein Rich Foods: 2 Servings Daily

1. Serving = 2½ oz (70 g) fish, poultry, game, lean meat; 2 eggs, 2¼ oz (60 g) cheese, 3½ oz (100 g) beans.

Weekly Plan (14 Meals)

The aim each week is to include the following items:

- Three or more servings of fish; two servings should be cold-water fish.

- Two or more servings of lean meat from poultry or game.

- Two servings maximum of lean red meat (beef or pork).

- Two vegetarian meals, such as pasta, beans, nuts, an omelette or a cheese dish; no fish, poultry or meat of any sort.

Why these food groups?

Follow this eating plan for life and you will do fine. It is designed so that if you fall short of your allowance on any particular day, you can make up for it the next day. Just be mindful that regular shortfalls add up, and so do excesses. Let's look at what each group does.

Fruits and vegetables provide important soluble fibre, necesary vitamins and minerals, and some protector substances that don't have the status of nutrients.

Grains and cereals provide essential hard fibre and add variety to the type of fibre in your diet.

Together, these first two groups produce regularity. They provide the correct fibre balance. They also increase the complex carbohydrates in your diet and moderate any sugars; this builds energy and stamina. A high fibre cereal should provide 4 grams of fibre per serving.

Natural bulbs (condiments) provide materials that help prevent cancer, high blood pressure and heart disease, and prevent minor infections.

Dairy products provide the minerals calcium and magnesium and are a source of protein. Dairy foods are most often short in a person's diet. If you don't get enough servings of dairy products, then calcium-magnesium supplements are essential. Also, increase your protein-food servings either in size or number. For example, if you include in your diet 50% less dairy products than recommended, add another serving of a high-protein food.

Protein-rich foods provide an essential tissue-building material for your body.

I have designed the weekly balance of these foods to meet the three conditions I set out on page 23 and especially to be sure you get enough essential oils. These oils are indispensable for your immune system, they help control inflammation and recent research suggests they protect against cancer.

A day for better health

I've planned a day for you according to the diet for better health, as an example of what you could do yourself. There is nothing special about it.

I've assumed you are like most people: you work for a living and don't have much time to prepare food. It is set out on the next page.

Most women will recognise that they would slowly lose weight on the calorie intake given, while men would lose it faster. In reality neither sex would lose weight because this menu doesn't include an allowance for sauces salad dressings, preserves, sugar on breakfast cereal or in drinks etc. Also, we have a tendency to adjust our portions to our calorie needs, so men will eat more and women less.

I chose this menu to illustrate some points.

- Breakfast meets three criteria: cereal, dairy products and a serving of fruit. The slice of wholemeal toast starts the day with some hard fibre.

- Mid-morning snack solves a second need: more grain. If a spread is needed, use marmalade in place of butter. Fruit is an alternative.

- Lunch is purposely heavy. I picked it because it illustrates that a business lunch is okay. A second choice would be a tuna fish sandwich without mayonnaise with similar accompaniments. Note that vegetables and fruit were included.

- An afternoon snack including another yogurt provides protein. Another choice would be some fruit or cheese, or wholegrain bread.

- Dinner is vegetarian. Notice tomato sauce provides the coloured vegetable and would normally include some garlic, shallots, parsley and other good things. Grated carrots are a secret for good sauce flavouring and are hard to beat for protector substances. The mushrooms add protein, and are an excellent source of other vitamins and minerals. The salad and green peppers provide other nutrients. The fruit dessert provides fibre, while the cheese provides protein and much needed calcium.

- A television snack can be healthy and refreshing. A glass of wine completes the day.

The glass of wine emphasises a point I made before: don't waste calories! I purposely didn't waste calories on fatty desserts or fried foods, etc. at other meals. I saved calories so I could savour them as a glass of wine in the quiet of the evening. You can see the calories for the day total just under 1,500. That leaves about 135 calories for a little salad dressing, a small amount of butter with my toast or a little sugar in my coffee.

Sample menu

	Approximate calories
BREAKFAST	
• Oatmeal porridge with bran or a 'bran' cereal with low-fat or non-fat milk and 1-teaspoon sugar	125
• An orange or half a grapefruit	65
• One slice of wholemeal toast	60
• Coffee or tea with milk	
MID-MORNING BREAK	
• Wholewheat roll (an alternative is a banana or another piece of fresh fruit)	60
• Tea with milk	
LUNCH	
• Small salad	50
• Fillet of sole grilled with shallots and slivered almonds	100
• Serving of lima or butter beans and rice	150
• A pear or other fruit for dessert	60
• Coffee or tea with milk	
AFTERNOON SNACK	
• Yogurt (plain or fruit), banana	100
• Tea with milk	
DINNER	
• Pasta; tomato sauce with mushrooms, garlic, finely chopped onions and grated carrots	215
• Small salad with green peppers	60
• Broccoli	25
• Fruit and a little cheese for dessert	135
TELEVISION SNACK	
• Apple, thin slice of cheese	185
• White wine (1 glass)	75
Total calories	**1,465**

Now we're ready for a short course in nutrition.

Protein

When you look in the mirror, most of what you see is protein. Your surface skin is primarily protein. You are about 65% water, 22% fat and 12 to 15% protein. Fat is nature's energy reserve for tough times, but people can excel with much less body-fat. However, if your protein declined by 10%, you would be seriously sick; if it dropped a little more, you would be dead.

Protein is the basis for every body-tissue; your body makes it into many forms and structures. The clear lens of your eye, tendons, fingernails, hair and skin are all variations of the same protein. Without enough protein, children can't develop either physically or mentally. Without enough protein, adults can't thrive. Protein is essential because our body keeps replacing itself. For example, your intestines get replaced about every three weeks, while your heart tissue takes months. Some brain cells never get replaced, so treat them well. While you read this paragraph, your body made about 150,000 new red-blood cells! And protein was the main component needed for each one.

Besides ensuring normal body replenishment, protein is the first thing called for when you are hurt. It helps your body rebuild the injured part.

Protein is built from 22 small building-blocks called amino-acids. We can make all except eight of these in our body. The eight we can't make are essential and we must get them in food; the others are non-essential. Proteins containing the right amounts of the essential amino-acids are of a higher quality than those proteins with some missing.

The highest-quality protein comes from animals. That's why eggs, dairy products, meat, fish and poultry are excellent sources. Most vegetable sources lack one or two of the essential amino-acids and therefore are of lesser quality. However, that shortfall is easily made up by eating a variety of foods; for example, a glass of milk with a meal of beans.

Protein and fat Protein and fat usually go together in our diets because we eat red meat and dairy products. The fat in these foods is saturated fat. One healthy eating objective is to reduce your intake of saturated fat. The Longevity Diet achieves this. Vegetable food sources almost never contain fat. White meat from poultry or fish and red meat from foraging game are usually low in fat, and the fat they do contain is polyunsaturated. Polyunsaturated fat is more desirable than saturated fat. Vegetables, poultry, fish and game are the healthiest sources of protein and form an important part of our Longevity Diet.

Red meat (beef, pork, lamb) usually has more fat then we need. Processed meats are obscenely high in fat. They were developed long ago as a means of saving protein and energy without refrigeration for times when meat was scarce. This is no longer a necessity, and these foods have become too costly to our health to eat them any longer. Once in a rare while they are okay, but we shouldn't eat them regularly.

Vegetable sources of protein, such as beans, mushrooms and rice, are combined with carbohydrates. Nature doesn't generally use fat as an energy reserve in vegetables. Nuts and avocados are exceptions with their excellent oils. They provide good sources of protein, but are quite high in calories.

An excellent compromise is to use just a little meat in a meal, to compensate for any shortfall in the quality of vegetable protein. Great cuisines began as the art of making the most of what little meat was available and improving the quality of vegetable protein. We need to do this now for our health rather than our pockets.

Energy

Everything we eat gives us energy. Protein gives us 4 calories per gram, but most of it is used for tissue building; therefore, fat (9 calories per gram) and carbohydrate (4 calories per gram) are the preferred sources. To get energy from these sources, your body reduces them to carbon dioxide and water, similar to the way in which an automobile engine utilises petrol. Extra energy is stored as fat. Fat is the most concentrated source and the most easily stored type of energy.

Carbohydrate is the most rapidly used energy because it is already partly burned and contains some oxygen. However, carbohydrates aren't efficient to store. You will see what I mean if you compare two carbohydrates – for example sugar and starch – to two fats – butter and oil. At body temperature, both carbohydrates need about three times their weight in water to dissolve and for the body then to store and use them. In contrast, butter is soft and pliable at body temperature and oil is liquid, and they both move more easily. The body has no problem storing fat.

The body prefers carbohydrate as the quick-energy source because it is already partly combined with oxygen. So the body stores about 3 to 5% of its weight as a special starch called glycogen. One reason many diets produce a significant weight-loss the first week is that glycogen substitutes for the energy that isn't being eaten. The 3 grams of water stored with each gram of glycogen is simply passed as urine. By the second week of the diet, the body starts to rebuild its glycogen reserves and the dieter wonders why the weight loss has stopped. At this time the body starts on its fat reserves if calories are still restricted. If the dieter sticks to the plan, they will be rewarded in another week with some weight-loss from fat! It will continue after that at 1 to 2 pounds (450 to 900 grams) per week maximum, if dieting sensibly.

A good reason not to put on extra weight is that it is fat! And it is tough to lose fat because it takes time and effort. Each pound (450 grams) of extra fat means eliminating 3,500 calories from your food. Think about this as you read on and we will get serious about weight in Chapter 3.

Although carbohydrate is the body's usual energy supply, it relies on fat for prolonged activity. For example, if you walk or run briskly for 15 minutes, your body uses carbohydrate for the work. There's a simple sugar, called glucose, in your blood and your body starts using glycogen. But after about 15 minutes, your body mobilises its fat. It is as though your brain says, 'This is serious activity and it might continue for a while, so send in the real power.' Actually, your brain wants your body to conserve glycogen.

Maintain a brisk walk for 30 minutes, and during the second 15 minutes, 50% of your energy comes from carbohydrate reserves and 50% from fat reserves. Prolonged exercise uses 50% fat and 50% carbohydrate. Therefore, effective exercise should always continue for more than 15 minutes.

Carbohydrates

Carbohydrates come in three forms: simple, complex and glycogen. Table sugar is a simple carbohydrate, as are the sugars in honey, and there's also some in fruits and vegetables. Most carbohydrate in a potato is complex; it is a starch. Our bodies store carbohydrate in a third form as glycogen, or animal starch. We make our glycogen from the simple sugar glucose. A good comparison would be one or two pearls, a string of pearls and a net of pearls. Simple sugars are one or two pearls; starches come as strings, and glycogen as nets. In these health economics, a string of pearls is better than just one or two and the net is best. It is the same with carbohydrates.

Our body processes all carbohydrates into the simple blood sugar, glucose. The best way to maintain the correct blood-glucose is from complex carbohydrates, such as the natural starches and the simple sugars from fruits, vegetables, cereals and grains. And although they all become blood glucose and glycogen, the body has a much easier time if the carbohydrates are eaten as starch or simple sugars in a natural fibre-matrix. Fibre in food naturally regulates the entry of the sugars into our blood.

Maintaining a consistent blood-sugar level has one rule: choose natural, carbohydrate foods, such as oatmeal, pasta, and whole grain breads. Do this and your carbohydrate intake will be correct. So, you might ask, 'Does that rule out cake?'

No! Cake and even biscuits are okay if they're eaten after a meal that contains natural, high-fibre foods. These would include some vegetables, possibly a potato, and a source of protein. The flour in the cake is okay; it is the sugar that's not good. To use sugar, your body makes a hormone, insulin. If it makes just the correct amount, everything goes smoothly. However, when you eat sugar without fibre, starch, or even protein, an incorrect signal goes to the pancreas, the gland that makes insulin. When it gets the wrong signal, the pancreas makes too much insulin, which causes the blood-sugar level to drop quickly.

When blood sugar drops too much your brain panics because glucose is its only source of energy, and when it drops too much or too fast, the brain perceives it as life threatening. Anyone whose brain is panicked from low blood-sugar is irritable, hard to get along with and shows poor judgement; your brain signals to you to eat more food so your blood sugar will return to normal. When this happens often enough, the extra calories will slowly show up as body fat.

Fibre is a natural sugar modulator, so we will study it next.

Fibre

In our Longevity Diet we emphasised the inclusion of cereals, grains, vegetables and fruit – all of which are good sources of dietary fibre. There are two general types of fibre: hard and soft (or insoluble and soluble.) We need them in a ratio of about two to one. Hard fibre comes mostly from cereals and grains and soft fibre comes from fruits and vegetables.

Hard, insoluble fibre makes us 'regular.' We get it mostly from grains and cereals, but there is plenty also in fruits and vegetables. Starting the day with a bowl of cereal, eating whole-grain breads, and servings of grains at other meals is important. Easily moved, firm, and consistent, light-brown stools every 24 to 36 hours signal that you are getting enough fibre. Until you move your bowels this regularly, make it a point to increase your cereals, grains and fruit; then keep up that level of fibre or a little more.

Soft, soluble fibre, as its name implies, isn't hard and mixes well in water; it is usually gummy. Soft fibre is found in fruits, vegetables and beans; there's also some in cereals, especially oatmeal and corn. Soft fibre removes unwanted materials from our body. It binds; scientifically it adsorbs. It helps to slow diarrhoea and prevents watery stools.

A good balance of fibres reduces the risk of developing intestinal disorders including diverticulosis, ulcers, gallstones, appendicitis, irritable bowel syndrome, colitis, ulcerative colitis and haemorrhoids, to name the most common.

Good regularity also reduces the risk of many types of cancer, heart disease, varicose veins and other degenerative diseases. Fibre helps reduce high blood pressure, arthritis inflammation and diabetes. You will even look better, because a person who's naturally regular usually has a clear, wholesome complexion! These benefits come from the two types of fibre that the Longevity Diet provides in the variety of fruits, vegetables and cereals you are encouraged to eat.

While the Longevity Diet is designed to provide enough fibre, supplementary fibre can help when necessary. We need 1 to 1½ ounces (30 to 40 grams) total fibre daily.

Water

Fibre needs water. You need water. We can manage without many vitamins and minerals for several months; but we can survive only three weeks without water.

We are about 65% water. Our stools are about 65% water. Water is the vehicle in which wastes are eliminated by our kidneys. It is also essential for maintaining body temperature.

Drink at least four, full 8 fl oz (250 ml) glasses of water daily. This is in addition to the water content of your food and other beverages. If you exercise vigorously or do heavy physical work, you will need more water still. One mistake most people make is to satisfy their thirst with beverages that contain calories in the form of sugar or alcohol. They trick their brain for a few minutes; then they are more thirsty.

Dehydration occurs when you don't drink enough water. It produces confused thought, dizziness and headaches. You can't drink too much water; any excess is easily eliminated and it takes wastes and toxins along with it.

Vitamins and minerals

The Longevity Diet contains all the basic vitamins and minerals. Equally important, the essential minerals, sodium and potassium, will be balanced correctly. Variety is essential, because most foods are rich in some nutrients, but short in others. Variety smooths out these shortfalls and satisfies basic needs. They only way to make sure you never fall short in the vitamins and minerals stakes is by using sensible supplementation. However, a single supplement can't provide enough calcium, nor can it provide fibre; it won't replace the Longevity Diet.

The UK government lists vitamins and minerals by how much is necessary to maintain satisfactory health. They call this level the RDA (Recommended Daily Amount). The best supplement will have all the recognised vitamins and all the minerals except calcium and magnesium at 50% of the RDA. It will have some calcium and magnesium, but not 50% of the RDA; possibly only 15%. The reason is simple: you need so much of these two minerals that they simply won't fit in a pill that has everything else.

A basic supplement

Selecting a supplement is difficult when you don't have a guide. After all, everyone who sells them says theirs is the best. That's why I worked out the following table to explain what a basic supplement should contain.

An excellent supplement

Nutrient vitamin	Supplement amount	% UK RDA
A (RE*)	500 mg	67
D	5 mcg	50
E	5 mg	Not established
C	30 mg	50
B1 (Thiamin)	0.8 mg	89
B2 (Riboflavin)	0.8 mg	62
Nicotinic acid (Niacin)	10 mg	67
B6 (Pyridoxine)	1.0 mg	Not established
Folic acid	150 mcg	50
B12 (Cyanocobalamine)	1.0 mcg	Not established
Calcium	300 mg	60
Magnesium	75 mg	Not established
Iron	6 mg	50
Zinc	8 mg	Not established
Iodine	75 mcg	Not established

* RE- Retinol Equivalent

The middle column shows the amount of the nutrient you should get in a supplement. The end column shows it as a percentage of the UK RDA for average adults.

If you search the chemists and health-food stores for exactly the same supplement shown in this table, you probably won't find one. Don't despair; simply come as close to that as possible. You might find all the vitamins and minerals, except calcium and magnesium. Take calcium and magnesium as a separate supplement (see below).

The supplement should contain the nutrients shown in the table, in approximately the same ratios to one another; that is the most important criterion – that it be balanced.

Selecting a calcium and magnesium supplement depends on the number of dairy products you use and how much your basic supplement contains. If you get all the dairy products recommended in the Longevity Diet, and your basic supplement has some, you are okay. However, if you don't use milk, yogurt, or cheese, make up for it with a supplement that supplies at least 600 mg of calcium and 200 mg of magnesium daily. These two essential minerals should not be overlooked.

Is more better?   More of the nutrients can help if you are following this plan; compare your body maintenance with that of your car. Keep your car well tuned and lubricated and it will respond well to good fuel. Neglect it and you may as well use the cheapest fuel available. If you follow the dietary plan and use the sensible supplements outlined, you will do just fine. If you feel better using more of some nutrient, it is okay; after all, you are a unique individual and have your own needs. Be cautious with large amounts of vitamins A and D as they can be toxic in mega doses.

Summary

Eating for longevity can be fun, full of variety and improve your looks and your life expectancy. Keep a few rules on a card you can keep in your purse or briefcase, so you won't go wrong.

- Eat for bulk; an apple instead of a sweet

- Fast food is fat food; fried food isn't far behind

- Five fruits and vegetables daily; more is better

- Deep-red or green vegetables or fruit daily

- Fish three times weekly

- Cereal and grains daily

Natural foods are balanced in fat, protein, carbohydrates and the minerals potassium and sodium. If you eat a wide variety, you will get all your vitamins, minerals, and fibre. Just to be safe, you can use supplements. It is important, too, that you know what foods cause stress on our body due to a vitamin/mineral imbalance, so that you can avoid them.

Foods to avoid

Processed meats, including sausages and frankfurters, should not be eaten. Over 70% of their calories are from saturated fat.

Confections are all sugar: this includes sugary cakes, biscuits, ice-cream and other ices. These foods are excessive in sugar and consequently increase stress by making our blood sugar go up and down like a yo-yo.

Tinned vegetables are generally excessively salted. Choose either fresh or frozen vegetables instead. Tinning upsets the natural mineral-balance of sodium and potassium, which creates more work for your body to restore the balance. Tinned fruit is okay, but drain off the sugar syrup or buy tinned fruit in natural juice.

If fat is hard at room temperature, avoid it! That rules out butter, lard and some margarines. Learn to use even soft spreads sparingly.

Oils for cooking and salads should be chosen for the purpose. Frying is best with a mono-unsaturated oil, such as olive oil. Salads are best with either olive, walnut, corn, or rapeseed oils. For baking, try to choose flax-seed oil; if its not available, use corn oil. Avoid solid fats and shortening.

To put your diet for life on a firm footing, here is a list of dos and don'ts for you to use as a checklist. You can copy this on to a card, too, and carry it with you.

Do eat
Fresh vegetables
Fresh fruits
Cold-water, blue-skin fish
Pasta with tomato sauce
Pasta with fish sauce
Poultry: white meat
Natural cereals and grains
Garlic, onions, shallots
Potatoes, rice, squash
Game, such as rabbit and venison
Shellfish and crustaceans
Low-fat dairy products
Whole-grain breads

Don't eat
Processed meats
Tinned vegetables
Highly-processed cereals
Sweets and confectionary
Heavy sauces
Hard-fat spreads
High-fat dairy desserts
High-fat dairy products

Eat in moderation
Red meat
Cakes, biscuits
Ice-cream
Fried food
Alcoholic beverages

CHAPTER THREE

Overweight or Overfat?

Now you are ready to assess your body fat. Notice I didn't say weight; your weight can be fine but you can still be overfat. In this chapter we'll show you six body-types and help you to decide which one you match most closely. We will also show you how to decide if you're just right, overweight or overfat.

WEIGHT, THE SUPREME FRUSTRATION

Two of the most frustrating things people can do is to look to fashion models for a self image, or look up their weight on a height and weight chart. Neither one presents a practical goal. Fashion models have become taller and thinner for their heights during this century. Since photographs tend to make us look heavier than we are, designers use tall, skinny models to show their clothes. So, the image we're presented with is moving further and further from reality because our average weight keeps creeping up.

Weight and height charts compiled from life-insurance statistics are in concert with the fashion image. They express an 'ideal' weight as a function of height and are based on statistics of who lives longest. They impart the message that being overweight isn't good. Charts that show average weight and height are somewhat more reasonable and impart a more realistic image. Other charts require you to decide whether you have a small, medium or large frame and go from there. That works a little better, but too often we may have combination frames – broad hips and narrow shoulders – and so on. No person is simply one single type, not even models. That's why the tests that follow are important.

Body-fat test

Body-fat composition is the only truly precise index of overweight. Most experts agree that our body-fat content becomes a sort of 'set point' that we subconsciously strive to maintain. We have to work hard to lower this set point and then keep it down. The upper level of body fat is 22% for women and 15% for men. You are better off if your body fat is about 13% for men and 20% for women. Top athletes usually have much lower levels – down to less than 10% – but that's too low for average people.

Determining body fat is routine nowadays. It is done by being weighed under water and out of water. Because fat floats, it is easy to determine your body fat by subtracting water weight from dry weight. Then divide your fat weight by your dry weight and multiply the decimal by 100 to get your percentage of body fat. You can do it yourself but you will need waterproof scales. Make sure you wear the same bathing suit in and out of the water. If the pool is not deep, simply ball up or squat down on the scale.

The float test

As an alternative to the Underwater Test, you can estimate your body-fat by testing how well you float in a pool. Float on your back and blow all the air out of your lungs; then note what happens:

25% Fat: You will float
22% Fat: You can just stay afloat with shallow breathing
20% Fat: You cannot stay afloat without moving your hands or feet
15% Fat: You will sink slowly, even with lungs filled with air
13% Fat: You will sink readily, even if your lungs are filled with air.

Men should strive for a body composition that sinks readily. Women should strive for a body composition that sinks slowly when they exhale.

Body fat can also be determined with body calipers, used to pinch you in various places, and a weight-height table that gives a value for body fat. You can do this 'pinch test' yourself, using the directions supplied when you purchase the calipers; they're a good investment.

If you are overfat but not overweight, you know that all you have to do is convert some fat to muscle, by exercising regularly. However, if you're both overfat and overweight, you'll need to diet to lose the extra pounds and to exercise to build more muscle and bones.

Your body type

For this test you will need a well-lit room with some privacy, a full or nearly full-length mirror, a tape measure and the figure-type illustrations shown on pages 40–41. (Put on a bathing suit, underwear or something close fitting, or just go nude.) Now look at the six figure types and decide which most closely resembles you. Face the mirror and get a general impression of your figure. Then look back again to the book. Which one looks most like you? If you are overweight, it's difficult to tell, but try to look *through* the fat and make an assessment. The illustrations on pages 42–43 show the six figure types for men and women when over-fat – you may need to look at these to make your assessment.

Hips and waist measurements help   Now measure your hips and waist, then compare the two measurements. This comparison will help you determine your figure type.

Figure type	Comments
Curvey/Hourglass	Hips balance with chest; defined waist
Heart	Chest larger than hips, thighs and waist
Ellipse	Chest, hips and waist about the same; thighs and shoulders narrow
Pear	Chest and shoulders small in relation to hips and thighs
Straight	Shoulders square; chest, waist, hips and thighs similar
Angular	Shoulders square; chest larger than waist, hips and thighs

A general overview

Studying yourself as described below will help you to see yourself as others see you.

1. Stand facing the mirror. Place hands on hips and find the tops of your hip bones. Then drop one hand width down and you should have about 1 in (2.5 cm) of padding on each side. Any more padding than that is excess fat which you have got to take off.

(continued on page 44)   **39**

FIND YOUR FIGURE TYPE

WOMEN

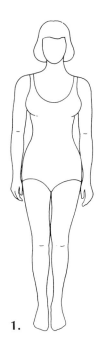
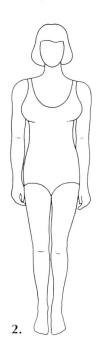

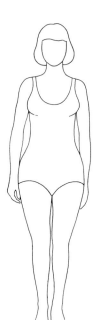
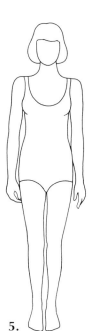

1. CURVEY/HOURGLASS
2. HEART
3. ELLIPSE

1.
2.
3.

4. PEAR
5. STRAIGHT
6. ANGULAR

4.
5.
6.

MEN

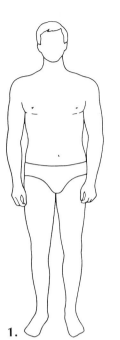
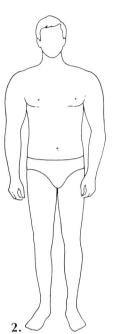
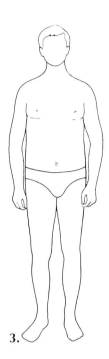

1. CURVEY
2. HEART
3. ELLIPSE

1. 2. 3.

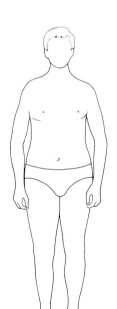
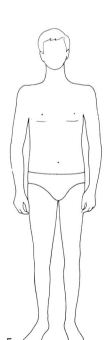
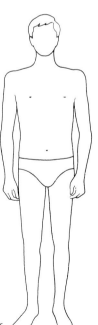

4. PEAR
5. STRAIGHT
6. ANGULAR

4. 5. 6.

THE LOOK OF FAT

How the six figure types distribute excess fat

WOMEN

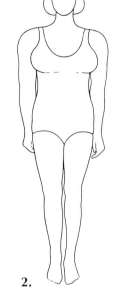
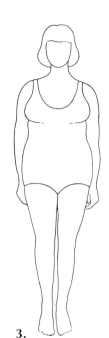

1. CURVEY/HOURGLASS
2. HEART
3. ELLIPSE

1.

2.

3.

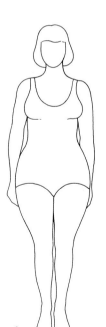
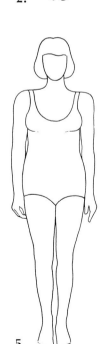
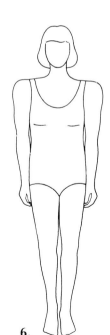

4. PEAR
5. STRAIGHT
6. ANGULAR

4.

5.

6.

MEN

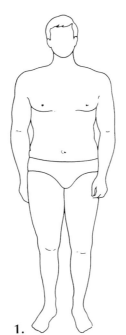

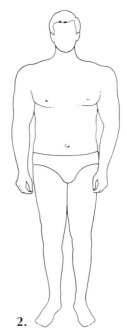

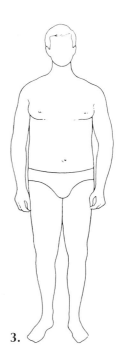

1. CURVEY
2. HEART
3. ELLIPSE

1.

2.

3.

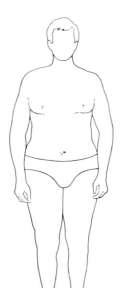

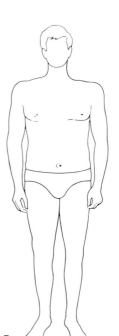

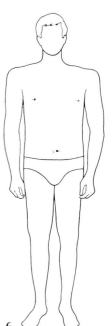

4. PEAR
5. STRAIGHT
6. ANGULAR

4.

5.

6.

2. Now with your feet together, look at your knees. Does a crack of light show through above and below your knees? If yes, great; if no, note that you've got to narrow those thighs down. Pear and curvey/hourglass shapes will have the most difficult time here.

3. Now look at your neck – do you have a neck? A long slender neck and well-squared shoulders tell you that you are most likely on the angular side and can be slender. If you have no visible neck or a short one, you are likely to be on the curvey/hourglass side, and will always have a broad, heavy body with rounded lines.

4. Look at your stomach – from just below your breasts (for men and women) to above your crotch. Is it flat, or does it jut out in a bulbous mass of flesh? It is probably something in-between.

5. Turn sideways. Look again at the stomach. Is it flat or do you look pregnant? Any body type can have a flat stomach. Your abdomen is likely to be more rounded if you don't have a long slender neck; the two seem to go together. Men fail this test more than women, because a male paunch is accepted in our society even though it shouldn't be.

6. While standing sideways, look at your chest. Notwithstanding the breasts, which may be large, you can get a feeling for firmness whether you're a man or a woman. Is there a fold of fat around the ribs just above the level of the elbow? Do the breasts carry excess fat? (Don't confuse sagging with fat.) Note these things because they will be the measure of your success in losing weight.

7. Now look at your buttocks. Squeeze them; are they firm? Make a muscle of your buttocks and squeeze them again. If they are soft at all times, you've got some weight to lose.

A final assessment   Stand in front of the mirror one more time and slowly look at the body you see. Is it, in your opinion, about right – cracks of light above and below the knees, stomach flat, no loose rolls of fat?

After asking these specific questions, make a general assessment. Is the body you see fat? If so, how fat – a lot, soft fat or just somewhat over-weight? Don't be concerned about firmness at this point; just attempt to decide on fatness. If you are a man and have a 'gut', which from the side suggests you might be expecting, you're fat! Resolve to bring it into line – we'll show you how.

LEAN BODY-MASS

As we have explained, if you are overweight, it's because your body is overfat. Or conversely, your lean body-mass is too low for your weight. Lean body-mass (LBM) is your muscles, bones and other tissues that have no fat. So when you are overfat, you either have to increase muscle size or lose some fat, or do both.

If your body composition is right, your weight will be correct for your height and build. For average people who work and maintain a good level of fitness, 15% fat is about right for men and 22% fat is the upper limit for women. Your LBM should be 85% of body weight for men and 78% for women. Take a 5 ft 6 in (1.7 m) woman at various times in her life. Let's assume she keeps her weight at 9 st 4 lb or 130 lb (59 kg).

Table 1: Weight distribution

Age	Total Weight	% Fat	% L.B.M.	Ideal Weight
20	9 st 4 lb/130 lb (59 kg)	22	78	9 st 4 lb/130 lb (59 kg)
35	9 st 4 lb/130 lb (59 kg)	26	74	8 st 11 lb/123 lb (56 kg)
45	9 st 4 lb/130 lb (59 kg)	28	72	8 st 8 lb/120 lb (54 kg)

At age 20, this woman was at university, 'on the go', active in sports and always busy. At 35, she had become a housewife with two children. While her weight was fine at age 20, she was overweight at age 35 and more over-weight at age 45 when the children were grown up and she had more time to relax. Even though she has been conscientious and gained no weight, she has noticed an increase in her hips, buttocks, thighs and under her arms. She feels fat, even though the scale says she is the same weight.

This woman faces a dilemma. She has been very careful not to gain weight and yet we are saying she is overfat. What can she do?

She can either lose fat or increase muscle mass. Her best course is to do both. The healthy way is for her to drop a little fat *and* increase muscle mass. Losing fat will increase her life expectancy by reducing her risk of cancer and heart disease. Gaining muscle mass will prevent brittle bones as she gets older. More importantly, more LBM will increase her basal metabolsim.

Basal metabolic rate (BMR)

Calories are the unit that measures energy, like centimetres and inches measure length and grams and pounds measure weight. We can look up how many calories are in a pat of butter or how many calories you burn when you run around the block.

If you eat more calories than you burn, you get fat. If you burn more calories than you eat, you lose weight. Gaining weight in our world is too easy because food is plentiful and we don't spend much energy on our normal daily activities even if we've got a job that requires some physical work. For example, an 8 st 13 lb/125 lb (56.7 kg) woman can get along well on 1,800 calories per day. Of that 1,800 calories, about 1,200 go to maintaining the basal metabolic rate (BMR – the energy required by your body to perform normal bodily functions).

Think about it; if you sleep, your heart still beats, your temperature remains at 98.6 F (37° C), your kidneys produce urine, you dream and so on. When these functions stop, you are dead! So, if this woman burns 1,200 calories as BMR, that means she has about 600 calories to spare. Believe it or not, 1,800 calories is more than many people consume during a day and they are still overweight.

You can get a good approximation of your own total daily energy requirement in calories by doing the following simple calculations. You will need your own weight in pounds (there are 14 pounds in a stone). If you only know your weight in kilograms, simply multiply it by 2.2050 to give you your weight in pounds.

How much extra energy?

To calculate approximately how much energy you require per day in addition to BMR, follow the steps below. By way of example we will take a 30-year-old female secretary weighing 130 lb.

Step 1: Basal metabolic rate in calories (BMR)
Consult Table 2 opposite to find your approximate BMR in calories. The figure for our secretary is 1327.

Table 2: Your approximate basal metabolic rate in calories

FEMALE

Height	Weight*	Cals per 24 hours					
		Age 20	*Age 30*	*Age 40*	*Age 50*	*Age 60*	*Age 70*
1.57 m	110 lb	1254	1243	1211	1176	1137	1105
(5 ft 2 in)	130 lb	1339	1327	1293	1255	1213	1179
	150 lb	1423	1411	1375	1335	1290	1254
1.65 m	125 lb	1372	1361	1326	1287	1244	1209
(5 ft 5 in)	145 lb	1457	1445	1408	1366	1321	1284
	165 lb	1542	1529	1489	1446	1398	1358
1.7 m	135 lb	1457	1445	1400	1366	1321	1204
(5 ft 7 in)	155 lb	1542	1529	1489	1446	1398	1358
	175 lb	1627	1613	1571	1525	1475	1433

MALE

Height	Weight*	Cals per 24 hours					
1.78 m	160 lb	1819	1715	1660	1632	1573	1491
(5 ft 10 in)	180 lb	1915	1805	1747	1718	1656	1570
	200 lb	2011	1895	1835	1804	1739	1648
1.83 m	170 lb	1896	1787	1730	1701	1639	1554
(6 ft)	190 lb	1992	1877	1817	1787	1722	1632
	210 lb	2088	1967	1904	1873	1805	1711
1.9 m	180 lb	1992	1877	1817	1787	1722	1632
(6 ft 2 in)	200 lb	2088	1967	1904	1873	1805	1711
	210 lb	2145	2021	1957	1925	1855	1758

*Three weights are given for each height: the first is ideal weight, the second is overweight, the third is obese. A formula for working out your ideal weight is as follows:

Females – multiply every inch over five feet by 5 and add 100.

Males – multiply every inch over five feet by 5 and add 110.

(To convert centimetres to inches multiply by 0.3937.)

Note: Personal BMR varies from one person to another and can depend on heredity. It may also vary according to the environment: in cold weather the metabolic rate is higher to keep you warm; in warmer weather, depending on humidity, it has a tendency to be lower. The lower your body-fat content, the higher your metabolic rate will be.

Step 2: Physical activity

See where you fit on the Physical Acitivity table (Table 3 below). Our secretary would come under 'Sedentary' which gives a reading of 0.2 BMR. Multiply this figure by your BMR reading from Step 1. The figure for our secretary is 0.2 × 1327 = 265.

Table 3: Physical activity

Sedentary (sitting)	0.2 BMR
Light (teacher, salesman)	0.3 BMR
Heavy (nurse, worker)	0.4 BMR
Extra energy used:	
Vigorous exercise	0.03 cals/lb (per minute)
Moderate exercise	0.02 cals/lb (per minute)

Step 3: Energy lost to food

Whatever we eat takes energy to digest and utilise. Although experts differ, a good estimate is about 10% of your daily BMR. If you are upset for any reason, it's higher, but on average, 10% is a good figure. So the energy lost to food by our secretary will be 10% of 1327, which is 133 calories.

Step 4: Exercise

I have estimated two types of exercise in the Physical Activity table (Table 3): vigorous, such as jogging, and moderate, such as brisk walking. From these figures you can estimate how many calories you burn up in your exercise programme: multiply the appropriate figure from Table 3 by your weight in pounds, multiplied by the number of minutes spent exercising. Let's say our secretary exercises vigorously for 30 minutes: 0.03 cals per lb × 130 lb × 30 minutes = 117 calories.

Step 5: Putting it all together

Now put the information gathered so far into the following equation:

BMR **plus** approximate energy from physical activity **plus** energy lost to food **plus** calories used in exercise **equals** total calorie (energy) requirement for the day

Let's go back to the secretary:

$$1327 + 265 + 133 + 117 = 1842 \text{ calories per day}$$

Remember that the above total is only an approximation. Also, in reality our secretary would probably spend some time on other forms of activity such as doing housework, walking the dog, or perhaps gardening. Step 2 does allow for some extra activities, but, depending on how strenuous the additional activity and how long she spends doing it, she may be expending further calories.

Further examples

Now let's put all this information together in another two practical examples that you can relate to: one for a 170 lb (77 kg) man and the other for a 130 lb (59 kg) woman, both aged 30 who have moderately active occupations and who exercise vigorously for 30 minutes daily. Their daily energy expenditure is shown in Table 4.

Table 4: Daily energy in two lives

	170 lb man (77.1 kg)	130 lb woman (59 kg)
BMR	1787	1327
Work energy: Light (salesman/teacher)	536	398
Energy lost to food	179	133
Exercise: Vigorous for 30 minutes	153	117
Total energy in calories	**2655**	**1975**

From this, you can see that BMR is the largest block of energy used in a day. Also, notice that 30 minutes of vigorous exercise doesn't use that many extra calories. In fact, a brisk walk of 60 minutes would be better at 204 calories for the man and 156 calories for the woman. The object of exercising is to build LBM and not burn more calories. Now let's consider fat versus muscle.

Fat versus muscle

Fat tissue doesn't require energy; it is stored energy. The BMR of fat is very low. Let's look at the BMR of a woman at three different ages, 20, 35 and 45, who doesn't watch her weight and body-fat composition.

Table 5: Results of losing LBM

Age	Total Weight	LBM lb	Fat lb	% Fat	BMR (calories)
20	9 st 4 lb/130 lb (59 kg)	101	29	22	1339
35	9 st 9 lb/135 lb (61.2 kg)	96	39	28	1331
45	10 st/140 lb (63.5 kg)	94	46	33	1294

You will notice that her total BMR declines in proportion to her lean body mass; as she loses LBM, she also reduces the calories she needs to stay alive.

Muscle is active tissue; it's always burning calories. Fat is inactive; it doesn't require calories and it reduces BMR calories. Excess fat is added under the skin first, where it insulates and retains heat and therefore reduces the BMR needed to keep us warm. Consequently, BMR declines even more than the above example.

Your lean body-mass is like the engine in your car. The petrol you burn depends mostly on the size of the engine, not the size of your car. Petrol mileage for a loaded car is about the same as an empty car until you load it up to the point where you have the engine running at full speed just to make it go. Heavy people spend even less energy exercising than you would expect from the extra weight they carry. It is because their lean body-mass – like the car engine – is smaller and well insulated to save heat. So, they get by with even less energy than a person with the same LBM, but without the fat. Research has shown that fat people learn to get through life with less energy. They learn to move slowly – find the least energetic route by taking the lift or bus – and when they participate in sports, they learn to use less motion than lean people. It's called adaptation.

Lose fat, gain muscle

Losing weight won't help the 35 or 45 year-old woman in Table 5, unless she simply wants to get down to 22% fat. If so, she'll be skinny and look haggard. People will tell her she looks tired; she will seem to shrink. The best course for her is to gain muscle and lose fat; then she could maintain the same weight and do just fine.

This woman's fat will have accumulated in a very typical pattern. First, at the back of the thighs; then, outside the thighs, the hips and midriff; and finally, in the upper body, especially under her arms. Long before this, she also noticed some lumpy areas, cellulite, on her thighs. She may have even spent some hard earned money on cures for the cellulite, which never quite worked. This pattern hasn't changed in 10,000 years! There is only one thing to do: lose fat, gain muscle and increase bone density.

Last in, first out

Your body manages excess fat with a simple principle: the most recent fat added is the first fat you lose when you diet or exercise. It makes a lot of sense if you think of primitive people living in times of scarcity.

Fat is added first in the areas where it is most easily carried. Therefore, recently added fat is the most difficult body fat to carry. It is logical to burn this most recent fat first, since its loss will do the most good. But while this strategy serves a body well in the wild, it's tough in our civilised, affluent world. Leaving fat in one area for a long time makes achieving a new shape difficult. It also causes the unsightly deposits we call cellulite.

Let's take a look at our six body-types again when they are carrying extra weight in the form of fat (pages 42–43). Notice that body-types one, three and four carry the weight worst, while type five carries it best.

This illustrates that everyone doesn't put on weight in the same place. Your body puts weight on according to its type. Therefore, some people get heavy around the buttocks (type four), the middle (type three), while others simply get bigger from the waist upwards (types two and six). Type five will put on weight all over. Most people can also put weight on the front of the abdomen. We call it a paunch and it seems to strike men more than women.

What our illustration doesn't show is serious overweight; where you've gained 22 lb (1 st 8 lb/10 kg) or 28 lb (2 st/12.7 kg). This doesn't require figures or drawings. If you are carrying that amount of excess weight, you know it. However, go back to the mirror and make an assessment. Then get to work on a plan to lose any excess weight you see there.

Look at the figures again and you will see where weight is added. It usually starts in the upper legs, back to front, then in the hips and finally in the upper body. If you are overweight, you know your body type, so you can see how the weight looks and that it will come off in the reverse pattern of how it went on. Remember, last on is first off!

Dieting and exercise together are essential. The objective is to add muscle while reducing fat. A pound (0.5 kg) of excess fat represents 3,500 calories. If you want to lose it, you've got to create a deficit of 3,500 calories. Ten pounds (4.5 kg) requires 35,000 calories! Let's go to another example. Just consider a 30-year-old teacher who should be 130 lb (9 st 4 lb/59 kg) but weighs 140 lb (10 st/63.5 kg). And suppose she is not exercising.

A realistic diet would be for this woman to reduce her food consumption to 1,000 calories daily and add 150 calories worth of exercise daily. This would create a total daily deficit of 750 calories. At 750 calories daily, it would take 46 days (about 1½ months) for her to reach her target weight.

Realistically, you can't maintain a dietary plan as tightly as this every day for 1½ months. Studies show that it is unlikely that she will be able to follow the diet for more than 80% of the time. Therefore, the plan will require about 60 days. However, the exercise will accelerate her change, because she will lose fat and gain muscle.

Exercise

Gaining muscle is easy: exercise! That's right; it is the only way and it is not as hard as you think. (The next chapter is devoted to exercise, but this much information is essential here.) Working at weights, starving, and torturing yourself in general, is not what's required. A simple daily pattern of aerobic exercise will start the process and you can accelerate as you become more fit.

Aerobic means 'with air'. Your muscles need oxygen from air (aerobic) to function; and as you exercise them, their need for air increases. The objective of aerobic exercise is to increase muscle activity enough to make them work, but not overwork, which simply puts demand on your muscles for oxygen that your heart can't supply. When you overwork muscles you lose muscle tissue rather than increase it. Overworking muscles is worse than gaining fat. There are a few basic requirements for aerobic exercise to be effective.

You have to exercise for a minimum of 20 minutes at first to start the fat burning. After 20 minutes, the muscles start using 50% fat for energy and you are on your way to gaining muscle and losing fat. You should keep the activity up for at least twice the minimum time and three times is better. Let me explain the minimum.

At first, the muscles burn only blood sugar and carbohydrate reserves for energy. Once the minimum is reached, the muscle tells the brain you are in it for keeps and to send in the reserve energy; that's when you start burning fat and it is doing double good. All exercise helps the heart and lungs, but when you do it long enough to start burning fat, you are building muscle at the expense of fat. In other words, you are gaining in LBM (lean body mass). The only other requirement is to keep the diet going.

Brisk walking, swimming, or cycling are good aerobic exercises that take 20 minutes to start working, so you should keep them up for at least 40 minutes and preferably 60 minutes.

Jogging, running, and rowing are excellent aerobic exercises that take 15 minutes to start working, so you should continue them for 30 minutes.

Jumping rope (skipping) is more aggressive and will start working in about 10 minutes, so you should keep it up for 20 minutes.

There are many ways of advancing from brisk walking or even easy aerobics. The walker can become a jogger, or better still, a walker with 'heavy hands'. Heavy hands are simply small weights you carry and swing vigorously to increase muscle work. After a while, you can purchase 'heavy feet' weights to strap around your ankles. Some advanced-aerobics classes also use these weights. The advantage walking has over jogging is that there is no impact on the joints. Walking is an excellent exercise that can be done by just about everyone and has no restrictions. And you don't need to go to classes to learn how to do it.

Again, let's consider the 130 lb (9 st 4 lb/59 kg) woman discussed on page 45. If she sticks with the Longevity Diet and starts an exercise programme, she will shift fat to muscle. That is all she has to do. It is only a question of where to start. I recommend walking or aerobics. Either one is fun, pleasant, and meets all the requirements.

Lose weight, lose fat, gain muscle

Our second example, the lady who gained 10 lb (4.5 kg) between age 20 and 45, has a bigger challenge. She has to lose weight as fat and shift some fat into muscle. Building muscle requires protein and eliminating fat from the diet is accomplished with bulk. We have already introduced the Longevity Diet, which will help you lower your fat intake and increase your bulk. Add the following seven simple rules to the Longevity Diet, start your exercise programme, be patient and you are on your way:

- No fried foods

- No red meats

- Only low-fat dairy products

- Two extra servings of vegetables or fruit

- No sauces

- No butter or margarine

- No dessert

The exercise plan for the woman who gained weight will need to be less intense, but she will still get good results. Her brisk walk might be a little less brisk and she should continue about 10% longer. She will be at her lowest level for a longer period, because she has got to reduce a little extra fat and add more lean muscle before the extra muscle can carry the extra weight easily. This will take about six weeks, by which time she will be down to about 130 lb (9 st 4 lb/59 kg).

Cellulite

Cellulite is a lumpy combination of fat, muscle and blood vessels usually found at the back of the thighs. The tendency to form these unsightly deposits is hereditary and often has little or nothing to do with being overweight, although excess weight seems to make them stand out. Millions are spent on the illusion that cellulite deposits can be reduced by massaging them with lotions or wrapping in plastic. Devices are sold to knock cellulite out with sound waves. Nonsense.

Cellulite is mostly fat. It will slowly disappear if you follow our plan and have patience. Look at it this way: you didn't develop the fat or cellulite in a month or two; in fact, it took years. Give at least six months to the programme described and you will find that the areas of cellulite are smaller. More time is required for them to become small enough so you don't care. Once you are down to your best weight and you are satisfied with your fitness level, inspect any remaining cellulite deposits. If they still bother you, see a dermatologist.

Spot reducing is another fallacy that deludes you into thinking you can reduce weight in just one spot. Often it is done by pounding the area with a machine or wrapping it in plastic. Then, after an hour or so, it is measured, and *voila*! It is smaller. All you have done is force some water out of the tissue. When the water returns, the measurements return to normal. Exercise will take time, but it works.

Dangers

You can over-do exercise. Many books have been written explaining how to pace yourself. If you have any concerns, I suggest you read a book written by an expert. If you are particularly unfit or have had heart, back or respiratory problems, do check with your physician first. However, the walking programme should be acceptable for anyone, even if they have had a heart attack. A good aerobic leader will divide people into groups to meet their fitness level and not overwork them.

Why we get fat

Carrying extra energy is necessary for survival. However, no one living in an affluent country like ours is faced with the spectre of starvation. In fact, the single, major health-problem among poor people is excess weight. So, getting calories is not our problem. The problem is that we get more than we need.

A major consensus of opinion has emerged among scientists who study overweight; it is called the set-point. This concept teaches that we adapt to a level of body fat and eat enough to maintain it – and it is natural to adapt to a higher set-point than a lower one. Several things favour an upward, mobile set-point.

Our BMR declines as we age; therefore, if you eat the same when you are 30 as you did when you were 20, you will push your set-point upward and gain fat.

Another problem is to do with heredity and body type; the figure-types illustrated earlier in this chapter accumulate fat in different areas. When we are very young, we develop the capacity for the type of fat we will have: we can have either many small fat-cells or a fewer number of much larger size. Then, depending on body type and bone structure, our genetic history dictates where the fat goes.

No one has to be fat. You can maintain a normal weight and body fat, but it takes more work for some than for others. If you have an angular body, extra weight hardly shows. If you have an ellipse-shaped body, a little fat seems to stand out. The main priority is to develop the right level of body fat and learn to be comfortable with your body-type.

Optimum health dictates that we do the best possible with our body. This means keeping body fat at the correct level. Good body fat might leave you with somewhat larger hips than you would like. That's life. Learn to like your body and be proud of its good qualities.

If you lose fat without gaining muscle, you'll look gaunt and undernourished. People will say you look tired. If you lose fat and gain muscle, you'll be slim, trim and healthy.

A final reward goes back to lean body-mass and the car-engine comparison. A lean body burns more energy because it has a larger engine. That means you can eat a little more without gaining weight. Finally, you will gain in stamina, because you will have a larger engine that can do more with less effort.

· CHAPTER FOUR ·

Physical Exercise is Important

Every organ and tissue in your body improves beyond normal ageing if correctly exercised. I said, 'beyond normal ageing,' because there is a normal decline that comes with our body's mortality and earthly gravity.

By exercising regularly and correctly you can gain and maintain lean body-mass at the right level. This will keep you from becoming fat and builds a reserve capacity necessary to reach your optimum potential in every aspect of life.

Exercise increases muscle mass, improves muscle tone, and changes its chemistry. Improving muscle tone is accompanied by better bone-density, which means stronger bones and slower ageing. You are also rewarded with a better posture and a lesser likelihood of osteoporosis (see Chapter 11).

WHAT KIND OF EXERCISE?

Aerobics are the most efficient exercises for improving and maintaining general body-fitness. Aerobic means 'air', but specifically, the oxygen in the air. Your muscles need oxygen to function and their need for oxygen increases dramatically when you exercise long enough. Steady exercise, at least 12 minutes for very active exercises and usually at least 20 minutes or longer for others, will produce aerobic conditioning.

Regular aerobic-exercise, correctly carried out, does more to tone and firm the muscles than any other type of exercise. It is the most efficient way to remove muscle fat and to increase muscle metabolism.

Pushing a muscle steadily for the correct time, such as jogging or walking, leads quickly to loss of fat and to good toning. Stop and go exercises, such as tennis, don't accomplish the same thing as quickly.

Non-aerobic exercises, such as weight lifting, take a long time to remove muscle fat. They don't condition all of your muscles, especially the heart. In fact, most strong weight-lifters can't run a mile because the general condition of their heart and arteries is often poor. Weight lifting is called anaerobic exercise, which literally means 'without air'.

Aerobic versus anaerobic

Aerobic means with air; anaerobic means without air. Of course, you do still breathe when you do anaerobic exercise, such as weight lifting, but unless you lift small weights in rapid repetitions for a long time, you don't exercise your heart and arteries and elevate your general metabolism. Your heart and arteries, indeed your entire cardiovascular system, are mostly muscle and require exercise more than any other system in your body. Fatty deposits in your heart and arteries are avoided and even removed if you do some form of aerobic exercise. So this type of exercise is the easiest way to prevent heart disease.

In contrast to anaerobic exercise, aerobic exercise works large muscle-groups, such as the arms and legs, challenging the cardiovascular system. In this way, major muscle-groups and the cardiovascular system are conditioned together. It is entire body fitness.

Obviously, aerobic and anaerobic are the two extremes of exercise. Aerobic is steady exercise of long duration; anaerobic is exercise of short duration. A comparison is in order.

Exercises classified by aerobic content

Aerobic (Long duration)	Stop and go (Intermediate)	Anaerobic (Short duration)
Running	Tennis	Weight lifting
Jogging	Downhill ski	Isometrics
Cross-country skiing	Football	Sprinting
Jumping rope	Calisthenics	Field events
Cycling	Handball	Golf
Swimming	Racquetball	
Rowing	Badminton	
Trampoline-rebounder	Volleyball	
Walking (brisk)		

Aerobic exercise, such as running, jogging, cycling or brisk walking, will produce a training effect (see below) for average people if done long enough. Running requires a minimum of 12 minutes while brisk walking calls for at least 20 minutes. These times are determined by how long it takes for your heart to reach a 'training rate' (which I will explain shortly).

Running a 100-metre dash, is less effective than prolonged running or brisk walking. It does cause your heart to beat very rapidly, but only because you have created an oxygen debt by using energy without air. You breathe rapidly because your heart and lungs are trying to 'catch up', to repay the energy debt you have created.

Weight lifting seldom causes your heart to beat very rapidly unless you create an oxygen debt as you can do in the sprint. You can convert some forms of anaerobic exercise into aerobic. A good example would be lifting a light weight rapidly up and down for about 20 minutes or more. But it is much better to jog, jump rope, or swim, because these exercises are far more effective and involve many muscle groups; not just one.

Tennis is stop and go. Unless you are very unusual, you have got to play tennis for at least two hours to get a training effect. If an amateur tennis-player gets a high heart-rate, it is an oxygen debt and not a training effect. Golf, in contrast, is a good way to ruin a walk. You walk, stop, swing, talk, then walk some more. Your heart never gets to a moderately high, steady beat to establish a training effect.

A training effect

This is scientific jargon for saying that you have done something that has exercised and improved your cardiovascular system. You have probably also helped to build muscles, such as those in your legs and arms, in the process. When you finish, you are a better person than when you started.

To get a training effect, you are required to:

- Achieve a training heart-rate (see below) quickly and do the exercise for at least 12 minutes; preferably 20 minutes. OR

- Achieve an increased heart-rate and keep it up for at least 30 minutes and preferably one hour. OR

- Combine the above two requirements by achieving a modest heart-rate and keeping it up for at least 20 minutes and preferably 40 minutes.

You should also do the exercise on five-out-of-seven days. Exercise is only effective when done regularly and with some rest-periods. Once you have been exercising one way regularly for a year, and are in shape, it is a good idea to use several forms of aerobic exercise on different days or weeks to improve. You will improve because each exercise has its own benefits.

Training heart-rate   For most people a training heart-rate is about 80% of their maximum heart-rate. Maximum is the fastest rate at which your heart can beat. Some well-trained athletes achieve the maximum during exercise under the guidance of an expert coach. But most world-class athletes train at 85% of maximum. So most experts conclude that if average folks get up to 75 or 80% of maximum, they are doing very well; and it is safe!

Training heart rates (for average people)

Age	Maximum	75% Maximum	10-Second pulse
20	200	150	25
25	195	146	24
30	190	143	24
35	186	140	23
40	182	140	23
45	179	134	22
50	175	131	22
55	171	128	21
60	160	120	20
Over 65	150	113	19

In the above table I have listed maximum heart rates and 75% of maximum to guide you. In the third column I have listed the 10-second pulse-rate you should aim for, so you can keep track of your progress. Multiply this 10-second rate by 6 to get your heart-rate per minute. Once you get into a regular exercise programme, you will only need to take your pulse occasionally to make certain you are not overdoing or underdoing your exercise. I have been doing aerobic exercises for years and I don't bother taking my pulse anymore.

What if you can't achieve 75% maximum?   Don't worry! Some people have a lower, resting heart-rate. If your heart rate is low, you are already blessed with a good cardiovascular-system; strive for about 90% of the training-rates given in the table.

However, there is one rule for people who don't get to a training-rate. They need to do it longer! The price for better than average health is to work a little harder to keep what you have got and even more to make it better. Look at it this way: you have got a precious gift that is worth preserving. Working harder can be running or walking faster, but doing it longer is better since you won't place as much wear and tear on your joints.

Why do it regularly?   To achieve collateral circulation. When you exercise regularly, you will notice that a difficult exercise becomes easy all at once. You have been making slow progress and suddenly real progress comes.

When you exercise regularly, new blood capillaries start developing. It is as if your body decides you are into exercise for keeps and wants to open new avenues of nourishment for your tissues, so it starts developing new channels to get oxygen-laden blood to the increased muscle-mass. These new channels take time to make and they open all at once. Think of it as a big, road-construction project where they open the new roads all at one time. It is like that with your body; suddenly you can do things you thought you would never achieve because you have opened new muscles.

The best aerobic exercise for you

Different strokes for different folks, as the saying goes. The best aerobic exercise for you is the one that you will do regularly, consistently, and long enough to achieve a training effect. Then you will keep it up for the rest of your life. Take a look at the following table of choices with a view towards picking the ones you like best. It lists three groups of aerobic exercise by the approximate time required to develop a good training-effect. In each category I have listed the approximate time necessary to achieve a training heart-rate and then the time for a toning effect. Less-vigorous exercises require longer exercise time and vice versa. Just about every exercise is listed and you can even modify most of them to meet your own needs. Over the page I go through each group and discuss its good and not-so-good qualities.

Typical aerobic exercises

1–1.1 min. to THR* (12 min. minimum)	3 min. to THR (30 min. good time)	8 min. to THR (50 min. good time)
Running in place	Jogging	Brisk walk
Skipping rope	Cross-country skiing	Bicycling
Jumping jacks	Rowing machine	Skating
Bench step	Aerobic dancing	Swimming
	Mini trampoline	

* Training Heart-Rate

Group One   This group is for people who are already in good condition. These are borderline 'anaerobic-exercises' that can be done long enough to get a training effect. If you haven't been exercising, you are likely to develop sore muscles from doing them. It is also difficult to exceed the 12-minute minimum.

Group Two   This group is available to anyone who is reasonably healthy. Some exercises, such as jogging and aerobic dancing, can be done in organised groups. Others, such as cross-country skiing and rowing machines, involve the use of equipment. The mini-trampoline or rebounder is a device that works well in a small room. Even jogging can be done on a machine in the home, office or gymnasium.

Group Three   Group three is the best starting-group for everyone! Heart patients can find a place here and paraplegics can do 'wheelchair' workouts. You can bicycle in the country or on a stationary exercise bicycle in your home. Either ice- or roller-skating works well. They can be done in a group or solo. You just have to devote at least 40 minutes daily. Start with 40 minutes and work up to an hour. Forty minutes seems like a long time, but that is what it takes to get your cardiovascular system working at the right level.

Exercise equipment

Almost every aerobic, outdoor exercise can be duplicated in the home. You can even watch television while cycling, jogging, rowing, cross-country skiing, climbing stairs, and others. Technology has made it possible for everyone to become physically fit without leaving the house. A few rules apply:

- Never use motorised devices. The motor is spending the energy, not you.

- You get what you pay for. Studies have shown that the most effective devices are more expensive.

- Simplicity. The best devices require you to use your arms and legs actively. You don't need added heart monitors and other electronic gadgets.

I am frequently asked which device is best? There is no single answer. I rank them in the following order:

- Cross-country skiing: These devices put separate effort on the arms and legs. You work all the major muscles and don't 'pound' your joints. These devices exercise the arms and legs independently.

- Stationary bicycles: These require you to use your arms and legs at the same time. They develop resistance by air resistance as the wheel turns. The only minor flaw is that the arm and leg exercise is linked together. Therefore, they are not quite as good as cross-country skiing, because one exercise powers the other and the total effort is divided between the two.

- Stationary joggers, treadmills and stair climbers: These are excellent for the legs and can simulate hills or make the difficulty meet your needs. The only drawback is that your arms are generally inactive; in fact, less active than if you actually jogged or climbed stairs.

- Rowing machines: These can be excellent if they have an independent arrangement for leg exercise with a moveable seat. Most of them exercise the upper body very well and the legs get very little exercise. If you have got leg trouble or have lost use of your legs, you can't beat these machines.

Aerobic dancing

Some of us like to exercise in a group or under the guidance of a leader-instructor. Aerobic dancing, more commonly called 'aerobics', is the thing. It requires an instructor-leader who set the pace according to the fitness and physical limitations of the group. So, 'aerobics' are available for the most physically-fit professional-athlete and for people with serious arthritis.

You can have 'low-impact' aerobics for people with leg problems or who are seriously overweight. In contrast, when you are advanced enough 'aerobics' can be done with hand and foot weights to burn extra calories and strengthen muscles.

When to start

This moment is the beginning of the rest of your life, so it is a good place to start. If you haven't been exercising, start slowly; a brisk 40-minute walk is excellent. Then progress to brisk walking for 5 minutes; then a 1-minute jog followed by 5 minutes walking, and continue in this manner for up to 40 minutes. You can do the same with a stationary bicycle or any other device.

STRETCHING AND TONING EXERCISES

Every aerobic exercise programme should include about 15 minutes of stretching and toning. These are exercises that require you to stretch the tendons in your arms and legs. They should also force you to exercise muscles in hard-to-reach places. They can be as simple as you want or as elaborate as you need. Do each one 10 times at first, working up to 30 daily. These exercises are suitable for men and women.

If you are unfit, overweight, or have any heart, respiratory or back problems, consult your doctor before undertaking any new exercise programme or type of exercise.

1. SIT-UPS

With knees bent, sit-ups – effective even if only done part way – help to strengthen and tone abdominal muscles. Put arms behind head and try to reach knees with elbows.

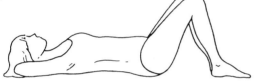

2. LEG RAISES (ABDOMINAL TONING)

Lying on your back, raise both legs, hold them up for a second and put them down. This tones muscles in the abdomen.

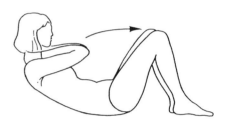

3. LEG RAISES (THIGH TONING)

Lie on your side and raise the top leg, hold for a second and put it down. Repeat with other leg, lying on your other side. This tones muscles inside the thighs and helps reduce their fat. Helps get rid of cellulite!

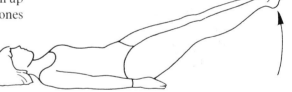

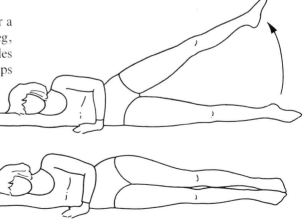

4. HIP ROTATION

Stand with legs spread. Touch each foot in turn with the opposite hand, coming straight up after each. This stretches lower back, hamstring and calf muscles.

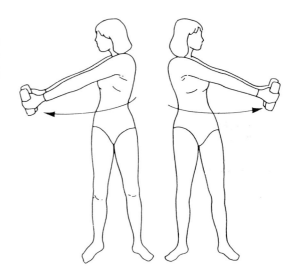

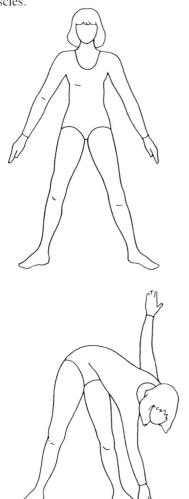

5. HIP REDUCTION

Stand straight, hold about 10–20 lb (4.5–9 kg) weights with your hands together waist high. Rotate all the way to one side; then back to the centre; and then to the other side. This helps reduce waist and hip fat.

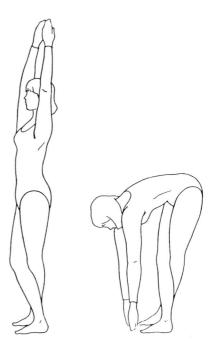

6. STRETCH

Stand straight, cross legs and touch toes in one sweeping motion starting with hands together high over your head. Then cross legs the other way and repeat. This helps stretch leg tendons and keeps them from getting stiff.

EXERCISES FOR FLEXIBIITY

Most exercise focuses on muscles and tendons, but doesn't always include the joints. So, to keep them limber and in tone, you should include flexibility exercises in your programme.

You can do these stretching exercises any time and anywhere, either lying on a firm bed or the floor; no special equipment is needed. One of the advantages of static stretching is that you become more aware of your body,

muscle tension, contraction and relaxation. These gentle and prolonged stretching exercises slowly pull and extend the muscles. Each stretch should be held for 15 seconds and built up to 25 seconds and repeated several times. Follow a progressive programme. These exercises are suitable for men and women.

Start by doing some slow, deep-breathing exercises (see page 70).

1. FULL STRETCH
Lie flat on your back with palms upward, in a relaxation pose. Pointing your fingers, extend and stretch your arms straight above your head. Point your toes and stretch your legs (making sure the length of your spine is making contact with the bed or floor) and tuck your chin in.

Feel the stretch throughout your body, head, neck, shoulders, upper back and arms, chest, abdomen, legs, shins, ankles, feet.

Then repeat the stretch down alternate sides, in the same way.

2. ARM SWING
Still on your back, with hands extended to the ceiling, slowly swing your hands and arms until they are flat on the mattress or floor above your head, stretching as far as is comfortable. This is a good stretch for shoulders and chest muscles.

3. KNEE CLASPS

Remaining on your back, clasp your left knee with both hands and draw it towards your chest, pulling and holding it for a few seconds. Repeat the same movement with your right knee, then both together to stretch the lower back, the buttocks and the hamstrings.

4. BACK STRETCH

For this stretch, turn over and kneel on the bed or floor, your buttocks sitting on your heels. Place your arms at your sides and turn your palms upwards to face the ceiling. Tuck your forehead into the mattress, close to your knees. This stretches the muscles along the back.

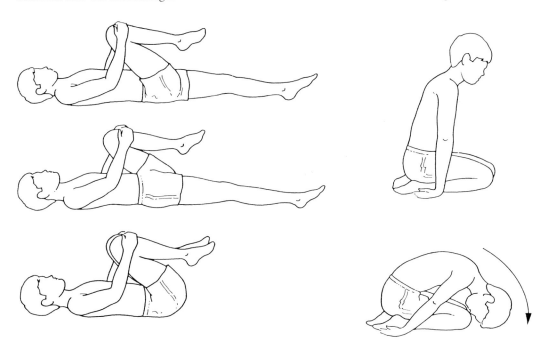

5. HEAD AND CHEST LIFT

Lie flat on your stomach with your legs straight and a pillow tucked under your pelvis, palms and elbows lying flat on the bed or floor and head looking straight ahead. Raise your elbows from the bed or floor slightly, lifting your head. This stretches your chest and abdominal muscles.

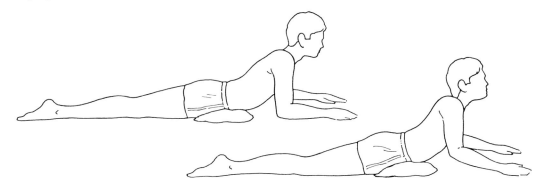

When to Exercise

Most exercise programmes fail from poor timing. Modern life-style is so complicated that both discipline and experimentation are necessary to find what is best for you. Here are some examples:

Nancy, a private secretary 'I get up at 5:30 a.m. and go to a 6:00 a.m. one-hour aerobic class. I need a group! Not only that, my schedule is so busy that if I don't get it out of the way in the early morning, I will have at least 10 reasons for not doing it after work.'

June, a Ph.D. research chemist 'I jog for 30 minutes at lunch time; then I do exercises for 15 minutes. I do it alone and don't speak to anyone. That way it is just me at my own pace.'

John, an editor 'I get home at 6:00 p.m. and go for a 30 minute jog in the winter or bike ride in the summer. It clears my mind and removes all the tension of the day. When I'm finished, the tension's gone and I'm at peace with the world. Even my children like me better.'

As you can see: Different strokes for different folks.

Is there a best time? 'Best time' is in the eye of the beholder. However, physiology gives the edge to the end of the day and sociology to the beginning of the day.

Exercise not only tones the body, it relieves stress and tones the mind. Stress for most people is usually highest at the end of the day, so exercise at that time helps the mind as much as the muscles. However, the difference is slight because there are indications that early morning provides a different advantage. Any time you exercise, your brain produces natural opiates called endorphins, which elevate your mood so you become more optimistic. While they help you feel better after the day is done, they also help you start the day with an optimistic outlook. So, while evening is biologically a little better for exercise to relieve stress, its edge isn't large.

Sociologists have learned that people who exercise in the morning are less likely to quit, because most people have control of the early-morning hours. You have only got to rise earlier and get started. Most studies have also shown that morning exercise makes you more efficient during the day. The efficiency is partly from an optimistic outlook and partly from the mental strength that comes with discipline. If you are typical, the morning is best.

Will I be tired? No! People who exercise gain more stamina. Stamina is staying power: the energy that lets you keep going after 10 hours like you were after one hour. Every study has proven that people who take regular exercise increase their stamina by a large measure over people who don't exercise.

Look at it this way: exercise makes your body and mind more efficient. Your metabolism is higher, but your heart works less to maintain the system. Your blood-sugar doesn't fluctuate, so your moods remain at an even level. It all adds up to being more effective.

A conditioned body also seems to naturally create an optimistic outlook. I think it is the natural endorphins at work and the confidence that comes from accomplishment. Studies have been carried out on professional race-drivers, business executives, secretaries, athletes, and housewives with the same results: condition your body and you condition your mind.

Everyone can exercise

If you have a chronic illness, such as arthritis or asthma, you must find an exercise that works for you.

Asthmatics can walk for 40 minutes to an hour to get the benefit. When the weather is inclement, they can walk inside a shopping mall or some enclosed area. There are also tread mills for using at home.

Arthritics can exercise in the water and achieve an aerobic effect by swimming for an hour. Alternatively, they can hold the side of the pool and kick with their feet or do the pool exercises below. When you exercise in the water much of your body weight is supported by the water, so your joints don't take unnecessary abuse.

In addition to these exercises, there are many aerobic exercise devices that can be used indoors. These range from rowing devices to stationary bicycles. The simplest is a small trampoline that allows you to walk in place. Gaining aerobic conditioning simply means maintaining the slow exercise for a longer time.

Pool exercises

Barbara has found the following swimming exercises particularly beneficial, coupled with the Longevity Diet. She could feel and see the effect they were having on her body within the first week. Her exercise routine also involves doing the breast stroke for about 20 minutes, and for the following 10 minutes a mixture of breast and back stroke.

- Lie flat on the water with arms and legs stretched to their extreme in a straight line. Then, in a scissor-like manner, try bringing your arms and legs towards each other, on top of the water. Then stretch and spread as far as you can. This exercises your shoulders, chest and arms, legs and outer and inner thighs.

- Hold on to the side, with legs floating on top of the water, then kick them up and down. Keep this up for the count of 30 to begin with, increasing it to 50 as you build up stamina. This exercise is wonderful for firming up thigh and calf muscles.

Breathing exercises

No one should exercise without first checking their breathing. Yes, breathing. But very few people breath correctly; do you? Look in the mirror and see which part of your body rises and falls when you take in breath. Does your stomach expand? Or is it your chest? If it's the latter you are shallow breathing and only using the uppermost part of your lungs correctly. Your goal should be to fill your lungs with air to enable you to get more oxygen moving around your body.

Learning to breathe correctly helps you to develop your diaphragm, strengthens all muscles connected with your breathing, restores energy, improves the skin colour and makes you feel more alive. Yoga schools of the East teach that to control breath is to control life force and perhaps life itself; we all know without breath we are dead.

- Inhale through your nose, at the same time holding your hands flat across your diaphragm and feeling the muscle across the bottom of your rib cage expand as your lungs inflate. Count to 10 while you hold the air. As you fill your lungs, hold your shoulders down.

- Exhale slowly, completely emptying the lungs.

Whenever you are feeling low, out of sorts or stressed, try deep breathing in this way; the results will amaze you.

· CHAPTER FIVE ·

Shaping up with Fashion

If you start on your Longevity Diet and exercise programme now, within a few weeks you will be looking and feeling younger. However, it's not instant. You didn't get out of shape, or out of condition, in a day or a week and it's going to take a little while to get every part of you looking and feeling 10 years younger. In the meantime, we can help you to recognise and emphasise your body's good points, and camouflage your bad ones, instead of despairing about them. Even when you've lost any unwanted weight or fat, you'll find the 'optical illusions' in this chapter invaluable as they will give you a well-balanced bodyline, whatever your figure type.

We can actually direct people's eyes to our good figure points and away from our not so good ones. Look at the diagram on this page for a few seconds. Which part are your eyes attracted to? Now turn the book upside down. Where are your eyes drawn to now? Do you think this creates an illusion of being longer? The broadest horizontal line will always attract your attention whether it is on a page or on a body. Where are you broadest – at your shoulders, waist, hips or thighs?

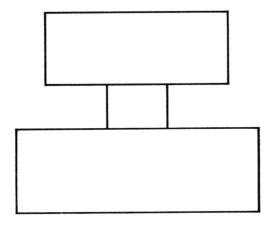

FIGURE TYPES AND FASHION

Now take another look at the figure types illustrated on pages 40–43. Which is most like your own? Note again the areas that are less than ideal. This will help you to recognise the style of clothes that will best flatter your figure and give it a youthful appearance. Clothes that have a good cut, and hang well from the shoulders, following the natural line of the body with ease, will always be flattering whatever your body type.

CURVEY (OR HOURGLASS)

These two figures (male and female) have balance between their top half and bottom half. The women are usually quite busty, the men quite muscular. This is a reasonably well balanced body, but it is best if women keep some of the softness of their natural outline, while men need to give themselves a slightly squarish look.

- When wearing shoulder pads, make sure they extend your shoulders past the thickest part of your arm, to allow sleeves to hang well
- Clothing lines should not be too rounded or tight
- You are prone to putting on weight around your stomach and chest area. If this is you, slacken your waistband or belt, and avoid tight or excessive folds or gathers of fabric below the waist

HEART-SHAPED

Heart-shaped women are usually quite busty, the men quite muscular. Both have broad chests and upper arm areas which are curvey (female) or muscular (male) in comparison to the narrow, straight hips, so they can look top heavy. Both need to bring the bottom half more into balance with the top half.

- When wearing shoulder pads, these should extend your shoulders past the thickest part of your arm, to allow the sleeves to hang unrestricted
- Wear raglan sleeves or line designs which make your upper arm and shoulder look narrower
- Vertical stripes, open-neck collars and designs which bring attention to the centre are best. For women, draped bodice styles make the bust look more in proportion.

If you need more bulk at hip level:

- Wear trousers and skirts that have waist pleats facing outwards
- Horizontal lines add width
- Generously wide trousers for men
- Fullness or drapes for women

ELLIPSE

Both male and female ellipse shapes have narrow shoulders and thighs in comparison to their thick waists. If this is you, your main area of concern is a thick waist. Make your shoulders look broader, to take attention away from your waist.

- Wear shoulder pads or clothes lines which give a broader shoulder line
- Straight yokes, wide collars and lapels visually broaden the shoulders
- Horizontal lines in stripes or patterns work well
- Keep the area below your hips narrow, by wearing trousers or skirts with pleats that turn in, to give a tapered look
- Avoid emphasising your waist. Women look good in blouson tops. Men look best in braces (suspenders) rather than belts

PEAR-SHAPED

Pear-shaped figures characteristically have full buttocks and thighs which do not balance with the slimmer top half of the body. In order to 'slim' the lower half of the torso, make the top half look broader by using shoulder pads and horizontal line detail.

- Whenever possible, shoulder pads are a must; they should make your shoulders appear wider than your hips and thighs
- Wear horizontal lines in stripes, or design detail *above* the waist
- Choose straight yokes, and wide collars and lapels
- Vertical lines in stripes or designs on the lower half of the body
- Avoid horizontal lines which end on your thickest point – your thighs

STRAIGHT

This figure type has straight body sides with balanced height. It has square shoulders and no obvious curves. Men and women with this figure type should endeavour to create broadness on the upper part of the body.

- Use straight shoulder pads which will give you an extra 1–1½ in (2.5–4 cm) width
- Horizontal clothes lines, such as yokes or epaulettes, will create width, and tucks and pleats can be used to add some curves
- Straight-cut trousers and skirts look best
- Necklines and collars need to have a straight look in line with the rest of your body, e.g. centre-straight detail
- A wide belt can be worn to accentuate the waist

ANGULAR

This figure type has a broad bony chest and shoulders that are broad in comparison with narrow and straight hips and thighs. This body is angular with no curves, so straight clothing lines are a natural extension to the body line.

- Wear jackets with classic notched collars, straight lapels and centre-straight detail
- If shoulders are much broader than the rest of your body, avoid big shoulder pads and never wear collars which point at your shoulders
- Raglan sleeves help to remove emphasis from broad shoulders. Eye-catching earrings, necklaces and brooches will also draw the eye away from the shoulders
- This figure favours vertical lines and design detail above the waist
- Horizontal lines and hip-line pockets will balance the lower half of your torso

Keeping things in scale

Your clothes should never overwhelm you, nor distract attention from you. They should balance and harmonise with your body type and colouring. The size of pattern and the weight of fabric should be compatible with the garment it is made into, and the size of the wearer, whether you are a woman or a man. Are you small, average or large?

Small If you have a fine or small bone structure, the line, patterns, details and accessories you choose should be small to average in size, giving a fine line. The fabric weight should be light to medium.

Average Go for the average in line, fabric weight, pattern, details and accessories.

Large You can wear larger than average patterns and lines, weightier fabrics, detail and accessories.

Style guide for women

Here are some simple but effective tips for women who are heavier, taller or shorter than they'd like to be, or whose legs are shorter, thinner or broader than their ideal.

Heavy women Don't try to squeeze into a smaller size; find the best fit (you can always cut the label out if you don't want a constant reminder of your size). Make sure sleeves don't pull around the upper arm and shoulders. Avoid short sleeves if you are busty, as these create a horizontal line making you look broader.

One-colour jackets, dresses or suits are slimming. Always avoid a break of colour at your worst points, or this will give you an horizontal line which attracts attention, and makes you look broader.

Keep jewellery and accessories good and simple.

Short women One colour outfits will give you height, so wear plain coloured dresses or suits or small discreet patterns to elongate your look. Choose jackets that are cut away at the bottom, to avoid the hem of the jacket creating a horizontal line and making you look shorter. With your jacket cut away, the skirt will look longer giving the illusion of longer legs – and more height. Shoes, tights and hemline in the same, neutral colour will also make your legs look longer.

Only wear a contrasting jacket when shoes, tights and hemline are all in the neutral colour and the jacket is short.

Avoid trousers with turn-ups which will create a horizontal line and visually shorten your legs. Also avoid shorts which end at the knee and trousers which end between the calf and the ankle.

Keep your accessories and fabric patterns small to medium scale. Avoid horizontal lines, frills and patterns at the hemline. Vertical lines, however, give the illusion of height.

Tall women   Tall, slim women should add horizontal lines to give the impression of greater width. This can be done by wearing separates, colour breaks, and designs with horizontal lines. Avoid jackets which are skimpy or too short. Double-breasted jackets look good as they create a horizontal line when fastened. Make sure that blouse sleeves are long enough.

Avoid one-colour outfits. Colour breaks will give you width and make you appear shorter.

Jewellery and bags should be large scale.

Hemlines   The hemline is a very important horizontal line, and it is important to experiment and find the most flattering hem lengths for your particular height and figure and when wearing different heel heights. Try and evaluate the effect created by the differing hemlines in relation to your figure image. Take it a step further: see how a thin same-coloured belt creates a different effect to that of a thick contrasting belt. Notice how contrasting belts emphasise the waist line and clearly define the length of the skirt. In all probability a short skirt worn with a thick contrasting belt will need to be longer than a short skirt worn with a same-coloured belt.

Legs   Perfect legs should touch at the thighs, knees, calves and ankles. The ideal leg length is one that looks visually balanced with the rest of the body. Your legs, ideally, should be as long as or longer than the upper part of the body (from the top of the head to the leg crease.

- While long legs are considered an asset, short legs need to be made to look longer, so match colour of shoes and tights with that of your hemline. Avoid trousers with turn-ups and very wide skirts.

- Thin legs will look even thinner in wide skirts; hemlines should end at the thickest part of the leg. Pale-coloured tights make legs look thicker.

- Broad legs will look broader still in very narrow skirts; hemlines should end just above or just below the thickest part of the leg. Choose very dark or black tights.

Style guide for men

Any male readers who feel this section can't really help them disguise their particular figure faults should visualise Cary Grant for a moment. How do you remember him? As a tall hunk of a man, with straight broad shoulders and a great posture? In fact, he was a tall, slight man with a big head for his body size. He used to have his suits made in Savile Row, London, with a 6 inch (15 cm) build-up to his natural shoulders to give him a great looking, well balanced body.

Heavy men If you are also tall, you will look best in medium to dark colours. Suits are more slimming than separate jackets and trousers, but if separates are preferred, keep a similar colour intensity for jacket and trousers. Waistcoats can emphasise a weight problem around the waist, so wear with caution!

If you are under 6 ft (1.8 m) tall, double-breasted jackets can make you look short legged and give extra bulk across your front. For a slimmer look, avoid side vents and turn-ups on trousers. Always make sure your shirt collars are big enough, and shirt buttons don't pull.

Wear braces (suspenders) instead of a belt (horizontal lines give width). Wear socks the same colour as shoes and trousers, or keep the intensity close to give you more height which, in turn, will make you look less broad.

Short men Suits will make you look slimmer and taller, as one colour in a continual line takes the viewer's eye upwards. If jacket and trousers are preferred, avoid a contrast in colour between the two, or repeat the trouser colour in a tie, shirt stripe or pocket handkerchief. Avoid double-breasted suits; they will make your legs look shorter and out of proportion. Remember that vertical lines give the illusion of height.

Shirt collars should fit well and not look bulky. Have short points and medium collar spread. Make sure sleeves and trousers are the correct fit and length. Avoid turn-ups on trousers as these give a horizontal line which will 'shorten' you. Wear socks and shoes of the same colour as each other and, preferably to match the trousers. This will give the effect of solid colour and so seem to elongate the legs.

Ties should end at the waist. Keep accessories down to scale.

Tall men You have the freedom to choose many different colours and styles, but make them appropriate to the occasion. Jackets and blazers look good on a tall man, and you can wear either single or double breasted styles equally well.

Shirt collars should fit well and look appropriate for the size of your head and neck. Ties should end at the belt buckle. Other accessories should always be to scale.

Horizontal lines emphasise width and can be used to visually balance a tall person by making them look shorter. Horizontal lines widen the point at which they are placed.

Particular problem areas for men and women

Necks

If your neck is short, wear narrow collars and low neck lines to create the illusion of a longer neck. Wear open or scooped necklines and keep necklaces away from the base of the neck. Vertical lines will make the neck look longer.

If your neck is longer than the ideal, wear high neck lines (polos, turtlenecks and ruffles), or high shirt collars to make your neck appear shorter. Scarves will have the same effect. Anything which creates horizontal lines will make the neck look shorter.

Shoulders

Shoulders that are visibly wider than the rest of the body and slightly square are ideal, as they balance the hips and thighs, allow clothes to hang well and will always carry body weight better than narrow shoulders, which will show every extra pound. So, if your hips or thighs are wider than your shoulders, camouflage them.

Made-to-measure garments and patterns allow for a 2 inch (5 cm) drop between the base of the neck and the shoulder line. If your shoulders have less than a 2 inch (5 cm) drop, they are called straight; a 2 inch (5 cm) drop is called tapered. Tapered shoulders always look much better when they are slightly padded to appear more square and the widest part of the body. More than a 2 inch (5 cm) drop is called sloping, and needs to be built up with shoulder pads to balance your hips and thighs.

Raglan sleeves worn without shoulder pads make shoulders appear narrow – worth remembering if yours are too wide.

CHAPTER SIX

Beauty is Skin Deep

We can make our skin look healthy and beautiful from the outside with oils, creams and other agents. However, what goes on inside our body, especially the effects of diet and lifestyle, has a more lasting effect on the appearance of our skin. By eating the right foods and choosing a good lifestyle, we will build a good foundation. Skin can always be supple with a natural, healthy glow, no matter how the years may come. So let's take a close look at what we have to work on.

THE LARGEST ORGAN

Accounting for over 6% of body weight, skin is our heaviest organ; it also covers the largest area. For example, a 120 lb (8 st 8 lb/54.4 kg) woman has 17.2 sq. feet (1.6 sq. metres) of skin, weighing about 7½ lb (3.4 kg).

Like all organs in the body, skin is made up of countless cells. It has two major layers. The cells in the outer or top layer of the epidermis are actually dead cells; the cells of the lower layer, the dermis, are alive.

Skin cells reproduce every three to six weeks; so on the surface you are never very old. New cells divide from the old ones at the base of the dermis, and migrate up as new ones are produced below them. As they move further up and away from the nourishment supplied by the blood capillaries, they are starved for oxygen from the blood and can't eliminate their waste products, so they slowly die and flatten out.

By the time these flat cells reach the top part of the epidermis, the stratium cornium, they are dead, but they still contain pigments and other materials: some of the materials you have eaten are eliminated in these dead epidermal cells when they are washed off. Like all other cells, they consist of protein, fat and carbohydrate.

The skin also contains many small sweat-glands which are connected to the surface by tiny openings called pores. Often a pore also has a hair growing out of it. The sweat glands go deep into the living dermis and can produce and excrete water when necessary. This water evaporates and helps to cool you off. In contrast, when it is cold, the pores close up tight to conserve body heat.

Skin contains a network of blood capillaries which supply the most important nutrient, oxygen, and remove the most important waste, carbon dioxide. They also bring to the skin everything else that gets into your blood. If you smoke, they bring nicotine and many other toxic materials. If you eat garlic, a sensitive person can detect it in your skin. If you use drugs, they will get to your skin cells.

Skin's responsibilities

Skin shields you from the sun, chemicals, bacteria and countless environmental factors. It is waterproof, so you don't swell up when caught in the rain, nor dry out when in the hot sun. With its layer of fat, skin is a shock absorber to protect your internal organs from damage and insulate them from the cold.

Skin is sensitive: a marvellous network of nerves in the skin, connected to the hairs, tells you what's going on inside and outside of your body. Your skin senses cold and adjusts your blood flow to conserve heat. Conversely, when it senses heat, the blood flow adjusts so the sweat glands in the skin produce water to cool you down with evaporation. Skin can simultaneously sense temperature, touch, pressure, light, air movement and humidity.

Changes in our hormonal levels profoundly affect the skin; so do alcohol, caffeine, nicotine, other drugs and our emotions. Skin reflects our mood; it tells everyone around us if we are angry or tense, stressed, relaxed or just feel good. It lets us know what's going on around us, and it also lets those around us know what's going on inside us. Many illnesses announce their coming via the skin before you even feel sick. A pale complexion might show a lack of iron; red nodules usually precede an intestinal upset; puffiness under the eyes can disclose a kidney disorder. But skin also reflects good health. When you are healthy, rested and not stressed, your skin has a nice glow, good colour, looks smooth, and is not puffy.

The sun and our skin

We need vitamin D to survive – and just the correct amount to thrive. It is essential for the absorption of calcium from food. Calcium is the mineral that makes strong bones and teeth, regulates our nerves and helps control blood pressure.

Cholesterol produced in our liver is carried by the blood to just below the skin's surface. High-energy rays in the sunlight pass through the skin and change the cholesterol in the blood capillaries into vitamin D.

Sun and skin pigment   Too much vitamin D is toxic, causing the body to deposit calcium in the soft tissues, including the major blood vessels and kidneys. Early symptoms are a headache, nausea, vomiting, and diarrhoea. If excess vitamin D goes unchecked, the victim dies.

How do we keep from getting too much sunlight? Our skin regulates the amount of active light – called ultraviolet light (UV) – that gets through the skin. Very light skin lets lots of ultraviolet light through and very dark skin lets very little through.

People native to the equatorial areas, between the Tropics of Cancer and Capricorn, have naturally dark, sometimes black skin. People native to the North, such as Scotland or Lapland, tend to have very light, white skin. Over long periods of evolution, the body has instinctively controlled its vitamin D with skin colour.

People who evolved in the temperate zones can develop various levels of pigments, called melanins, depending upon the intensity of the UV light. That is why native Italians develop a nice, dark tan in the summer and people native to the in between areas, such as Paris, France, have light skin, but can develop a moderately-dark tan. This ability to produce pigment explains why naturally fair-skinned people don't tan, but burn if exposed to excessive sunlight. When you do burn, it is nature's way of saying you are getting too much sun.

Sunburn doesn't generally happen to people living in northern areas because the ultraviolet rays don't get strong enough; the sun is too low in the sky. As sunlight passes through the atmosphere, the UV light gets filtered out; so, the lower the sun is in the sky, the less UV gets through. It's when these fair-skinned people travel south that the problems begin.

Dermatologists often classify skin in six categories based on sensitivity to sunlight; then they superimpose such terms as dry, extra dry or oily. (See pages 90–91).

Dryness usually goes with light skin, blue eyes and fair hair. Dark-skinned, dark-haired people have thicker, more oily skin. Dry skin is also a characteristic of aging.

Skin pigments and oils help prevent the skin from drying because the dead, epidermal cells are plump and form a tight, smooth barrier that keeps the skin moist, flexible and soft.

Don't eat a high-fat diet in hopes that your skin will become more oily.

Instead, focus on EPA, GLA, vitamin E and beta-carotene (see under *Dietary know-how* on pages 86–7). These oils find their way into the epidermis, helping it to remain supple and not dry out as quickly.

Also, vitamin C is essential for skin collagen, the protein that gives skin its strength. If you *don't* eat your serving of raw vegetables and fruit daily, an extra 100 mg or more of vitamin C can help.

Wrinkles

Age, excessive sunburn, tanning, smoking, working in a smoke-filled or air-polluted environment, and worry all cause wrinkles. This happens for several reasons, all of which can be reduced by good diet in addition to correct, topically-applied sunscreens. As we get older, hormonal balances change, gravity takes its toll, and we lose the ability to rebuild our collagen; consequently, there is a tendency for skin to sag and wrinkle.

Studies have shown clearly that smokers have more wrinkles than non-smokers making them appear at least five years older. Smoking puts toxic chemicals into our blood. It follows, that polluted air also causes wrinkles because many of the same chemicals are breathed into our lungs.

Skin is protein and since smoking interferes with the building of protein, we can gain insight into how the wrinkles develop. Smoking causes a reduction in the blood level of vitamin C which is necessary to make collagen. Smoking also lowers blood levels of beta-carotene, vitamin E and some minerals. These nutrient changes in the blood increase the risk of emphysema, a disease in which lung tissue loses its elasticity and becomes inflexible. Therefore, if you smoke, stop! If you work or live where there's a lot of smoke or fumes, take extra beta-carotene and vitamin E. This will help delay the onset of wrinkles and will also help prevent emphysema in your old age.

In light-skinned people, the UV rays of the sun penetrate to the living dermis and prevent correct manufacture of connective tissue. This can be prevented by getting more vitamin C and beta-carotene. If you are exposed to excessive sun and smoke, you should take vitamin C, vitamin E and beta-carotene as supplements to help counteract these effects.

Beta-carotene, 15 to 25 milligrams daily, helps modulate UV light and reduces sun damage. This protection by beta-carotene protects vitamin C, which is necessary for body manufacture of the correct connective proteins so your skin won't become excessively wrinkled and leathery. Vitamin E, 50 International Units daily, or about 400 IU every three or four days helps prevent age spots. These spots are pigments which accumulate in response to UV light, smoke and other toxins.

Of course, the best prevention for wrinkles, skin pigment spots and 'general ageing', is to protect yourself from the sun, avoid polluted air and not smoke. Since you can't avoid all these things, especially if you work in a city, the next most appropriate step is sensible supplementation.

You can also protect your skin from unwanted wrinkles by avoiding repetitive wrinkles. For example, 'crow's feet' that develop around our eyes do so because we habitually squint from the sun or smoke. Wearing sunglasses and avoiding smoke will help to prevent this from happening by stopping 'crow's feet' at the source. Similarly for frowning and other habits.

One easy way to help reduce the development of these 'habit' wrinkles is to relax the face often. It's easy. Simply close your eyes and force your face to relax for a full minute as often as you can in your normal daily routine. This brief relaxation will let normal circulation get to those areas where the wrinkle has cut it off and restore normal metabolism. If you can learn not to frown or squint at all, you will do even better.

Dietary know-how

There are a few other dietary ways to improve dry skin and delay natural wrinkles. Two oils in food are of some natural help. These oils are called EPA, short for eicosapentaenoic acid and GLA, short for gamma linolenic acid. EPA comes from fish and GLA from oil of evening primrose and blackcurrants.

The Longevity Diet in Chapter 2 provides enough of these oils for average people. But suppose you are not average and have dry, light skin; what can you do? Eat blue-skinned, cold-water fish (such as salmon, tuna, mackerel, plaice, anchovies) and use 'seed and nut' oils for salads and cooking. The best seed-oils are flax, sesame and linseed.

EPA supplements   Pure cod-liver oil or capsules of fish oil can add EPA to your diet. Select supplements that contain at least 180 mg of EPA per capsule. I recommend you strive for about 500 mg of EPA daily. On days you don't eat fish, that calls for one teaspoon of cod-liver oil, three capsules of EPA or 1 teaspoon of flaxseed oil.

GLA   Supplements of evening primrose oils or GLA supplements can be taken. A single capsule of evening primrose oil should be adequate.

Your diet affects your skin in many ways. If you follow the Longevity Diet, you will get sufficient fibre, vitamins and minerals. However, there are a few more things you can do to be sure your skin will look its best.

Fibre   You are getting enough of this when you have an easy bowel-movement of light-brown stools, every 24 to 36 hours.

Iron   Are you getting nutrition insurance by using the supplement described on the Supplement table in Chapter 2? Make sure you get at least 9 mg of supplemental iron daily.

Calcium   Are you getting 3 servings of dairy products daily? If not, take 200 mg of calcium for every serving you miss.

Beta-carotene   Follow the advice in Chapter 2 and get lots of colour on your plate. For extra insurance, take 5 mg of supplemental beta-carotene daily; better still, take 15 mg every other day. If you have light skin, blue eyes and naturally light hair, take an extra 15 mg of beta-carotene every day. It can do a lot of good and no harm. Beta-carotene, one of nature's most effective protectors, is a plant pigment that makes carrots orange and vegetables, such as spinach and broccoli, dark green. Our body converts beta-carotene to vitamin A as required, and the remaining beta-carotene protects membranes from environmental damage.

Fish oils   If you don't eat fish, take a teaspoon of pure cod-liver oil daily. Or, if you don't like its taste, take capsules that provide at least 800 mg of fish oil daily. That is usually 1 to 3 capsules.

I can't emphasise strongly enough the need for good nutrition. You wouldn't be using this book if you were not striving for optimum health. Therefore, you need to go further than most people. Look once more at the Supplement table in Chapter 2 to make sure you are getting enough of the basic nutrients. Supplements at that level will place you far above average in nutritional health.

GOOD, YOUTHFUL LOOKING SKIN

A youthful looking skin that radiates good health is what anyone would wish for at any age. But wishful thinking isn't enough, as you have just learned from James Scala. Even the very young, of course, do not always have perfect skin, but after 30 your skin needs constant care and attention if you want it to rate a second glance or touch. Also, your habits – good or bad – will determine how quickly your skin shows signs of ageing.

Try the elasticity skin test. Pinch the loose skin on the back of your hand and hold it to the count of five, then let it go. See if it returns to normal immediately or before the count of three. If it doesn't, your skin is ageing and losing its elasticity.

We have already explained how a poor diet, exposure to the sun, smoking and stress can and do cause our skin to sag, wrinkle and become 'old looking' prematurely. So it makes sense to adapt an anti-ageing programme.

A good skin-care routine (for men as well as women) does not take up very much time – and every minute expended is repaid a thousandfold. Choose good anti-ageing skin-care products that contain active ingredients to increase oxygenation in the skin cells and stimulate healthy cell renewal. This will give you a more youthful look, and help you feel good about yourself.

General skin care for women

Even those of us lucky enough to have good skin need to cleanse and moisturise it conscientiously. But whatever your skin type, the following routine works wonders.

Step 1   Use a good cleansing soap or lotion, to remove dirt and impurities. Afterwards, the skin should feel clean, fresh and 'renewed' – not stripped and uncomfortably tight.

Two to three times per week, or as required, use an exfoliating cream to remove dead surface cells and reveal a fresher, younger looking complexion. Alternatively, use a conditioning mask to stimulate blood circulation, moisturise and condition all in one.

Step 2   Use a refiner (toner) to clear away unwanted debris and prepare the skin for a moisturiser and protector. Choose one that doesn't contain alcohol, as this strips the skin of its natural protection. The skin then sends an SOS to the brain which, in turn, over-reacts and deposits more excessive oil on the skin's surface.

Step 3   Use a day-time moisturiser high in UVA and UVB protection, and preferably one that moisturises via liposomes which contain thyaluronic acid. This latter is a softening and smoothing ingredient also found naturally in the skin; this dramatically improves the skin's texture, firmness and smoothness within a few days of regular use.

Step 4   At night, lightly apply a replenishing cream to nourish and rejuvenate your skin while you sleep.

General skin care for men

Over recent years, the range of toiletries and skin-care products for men has increased dramatically, so why not join the growing numbers that find they really are beneficial?

Step 1   Use a good cleansing soap or lotion to remove dirt and debris without stripping your skin.

Step 2   Use the method of shaving which suits your skin and fits into your daily routine best. Shaving is good for your looks, particularly a wet shave, as this also acts as an exfoliator, removing the dead cells that otherwise make your skin look dull and flaky. Then use an exfoliating cream to clear the skin on the areas not shaven.

Step 3   After a wet shave, splash your face with cold water or a non-alcoholic toner to help tighten the pores. Then apply a soothing, non-perfumed moisturiser.

Dry shavers should seriously consider using an exfoliating cleansing cream as this will gently stimulate the renewal of skin cells, thereby regulating and improving oxygen absorption by the skin. The cream cleanses deeply, removing dead skin cells that otherwise make the skin look dull. Cleanse, refine and moisturise twice daily.

Know your skin

Whatever your skin type, it will have plus and minus factors – as you probably know all too well. Let's take a look at potential problem areas and see what can be done.

Oily skin   Oily and combination skins can be an advantage when you are a little older. If you have looked after it well, the chances are that it isn't showing its age. Even when we are young, an oily skin is more of a bother than a problem. You have to cleanse regularly, but if you do that conscientiously to keep open pores, blackheads and spots at bay, you definitely have an advantage over people with dry skin.

If, however, excessive oiliness has led to skin problems, follow the Longevity Diet and look after your skin in the following way. Cleanse your skin twice daily with a glycerin soap or cleanser, and as often as you feel comfortable with, deep cleanse with an exfoliating cream (or oats wrapped in a muslin pouch). Gently massage this into the skin to remove dead surface cells and reveal a fresher, younger looking complexion. Rinse well, then use a non-alcohol toner and a protective moisturiser. At the end of the day, use a night-replenishing moisturising cream specially designed for oily skins.

For mild skin eruptions, you could obtain from the chemist a sulphur and resorcinol paste, and benzoyl peroxide for home treatment. However, a visit to a dermatologist may prove to be worth while at this early stage, as there are treatments available which can prevent a small problem developing into a big one, and lessen or even cure more serious problems.

Dry skin   If you have a normal to dry skin, in your teens and twenties you will no doubt have had smooth, fine and spot-free skin. Then, suddenly, with a few added years, it is not as smooth or as clear. Without appropriate care this type of skin can become dry, with premature lines and wrinkles. It is also more prone to allergic reactions, broken veins, rashes and ruddiness caused by sensitivity to the weather and irritants.

Fortunately, it has tremendous powers of self-regeneration when properly cared for. First, avoid irritants you know cause problems and treat new perfume, toiletries and cosmetics with caution. Use only the mildest of soaps on your face; better still, a light cream or lotion-type cleanser, then a gentle (no alcohol) toner, followed by a skin-firming product that contains liposomes (anti-ageing ingredients to help regenerate and tighten the more mature skin). Then apply a daytime moisturiser with high UVA and UBA protection. At night, use a replenishing cream designed for dry skin.

Extra dry skin All skins, but especially dry skins, may benefit from cream or spray with a concentration of sodium pyrrolidine carboxylate (also known as Na. PCA). This moisture-attracting substance, naturally occurring in the skin, is commercially packaged in a refreshing spray mist which accelerates and re-activates the effects of your moisturiser. It also sets make-up, without giving you a mask-like look (and in addition it is excellent for resetting hair between shampoos!).

Once a week deep cleanse with a conditioning mask applied over a light film of moisturiser or night cream (as a quick 'pick me up' for dehydrated skins). For lines around the mouth and frown lines, use a cream exfoliator very lightly three times a week, or whatever your skin feels comfortable with.

Remember, too, that central heating and air conditioning are drying for your skin. If you haven't a humidifier, small bowls of water placed near radiators will help.

Also, follow our advice on diet and exercise, and flatter your skin by wearing your best colours.

Hydrated skin Skin that looks puffy or bloated is hydrated, through being clogged by toxins. Your skin is telling you that you need to improve your circulation, so that your body can function efficiently.

Facial massage and exercises (see pages 92–96) will improve the colour of your skin as well as your circulation, and help your body to rid itself of trapped fluid and waste matter. If the problem is extreme, a beauty salon treatment called 'Cathiodermie' facial treatment is very effective, or a dermatologist can recommend other appropriate treatments.

The benefits of massage

At 20 your skin tissue is firm, but lines may already be starting to form. At 30, foreheads may show frown lines and furrows. At 40, muscles begin to droop and sag. At 50, early neglect is apparent everywhere. So, it is never too soon to start pampering your skin – and, fortunately, never too late to see some benefits.

The facial and massage techniques on pages 92–95, suitable for men and women alike, were learnt from one of Hollywood's greats, the make-up artist Ern Westmore. He believed that whether you are young, middle-aged or older, you can become far more attractive, which in turn improves your self-confidence. Think about it, the results are far more than just skin deep.

To quote Ern Westmore, 'Why spend 24 hours a day growing older when you can spend those hours growing younger and more beautiful?'

FACIAL MASSAGE

Muscles in the face and neck can be toned with massage to improve the features they control:

- Forehead muscles control the appearance of the brow

- Eye muscles control the movement and expression of the eyelids

- Mouth muscles determine the set of your mouth and lips

- Jaw and chin muscles control the firmness or otherwise of the chin and jaw line

- Cheek muscles control the firmness of the cheeks

The following facial massage techniques concentrate on all these areas of the face. To see results, you really need to practise these techniques at least three times a week.

Facial massage is also a good way of relieving stress or tension in the face. To see how tense your facial muscles are, tell yourself to relax your face right now, and feel what happens. You'll probably be surprised at how tense your forehead and jaw were. You may even have been frowning without realising it – too much of which can lead to those unwanted frown lines.

Before you begin

Open this book and stand it upright on the table to one side of your dressing table mirror. Then look into the mirror and use the techniques given to firm your features and hold back tell-tale signs of ageing. Once you have learned these simple finger movements, you can give yourself a facial massage every time you cleanse your face.

Choose a time when you can be completely relaxed with no interruptions – perhaps before taking a bath or shower.

- Seat yourself comfortably before a mirror

- Apply a little cleansing cream to your already cleansed face and neck to help your fingers glide over your skin

- Always use gentle, circular movements, working upwards and outwards with your fingertips lightly playing over the surface of your face; never pull or drag the skin.

NECK, JOWL AND DOUBLE CHIN

Begin with the flat of the fingers of your right hand in a gentle pressing, lifting movement at the base of your throat. Slowly move your hand up your throat and around your neck and chin to your left ear. Then repeat, but using your left hand to massage the right side of your neck, chin and up towards your right ear. Alternate hands in this manner until you have carried out this action 5 times each side – or for as long as you feel comfortable.

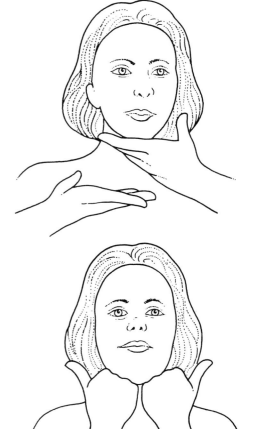

JOWL AND DOUBLE CHIN

Place your elbows on the table and cup your hands under your chin and jowl. Using your knuckles, start at the chin with gentle kneading movements, moving towards the ears, counting with each knuckle movement 1, 2, 3, 4 forward and then 1, 2, 3, 4 backwards. Repeat at least 5 times. Give your hands and fingers a good shake out.

LOWER CHEEK

Place your thumbs under your chin (in line with the edges of your mouth) to help steady your movements. Then place the first three fingers of both hands on the lowest point of each cheek and move them gently upwards and outwards in a series of little lifting circles to the ears.

FOREHEAD

Start with the fingertips of both hands touching each other on your forehead, above your nose. Use your fingers to 'lift' your forehead with light, upward strokes from your eyebrows to your hairline, gradually moving your fingers further apart along your forehead.

For horizontal lines, start with all the fingers from your right hand on your left temple or of your left hand on your right temple. Work them gently across the entire forehead from temple to temple, smoothing out any frown lines. Repeat both steps six times.

AROUND THE EYE AREA

Be very gentle; do not press too hard, or stretch or pull the skin. Press the middle finger of each hand into the inner corners of your eyes; rest: one, two, three. Now slide both middle and second fingers down underneath

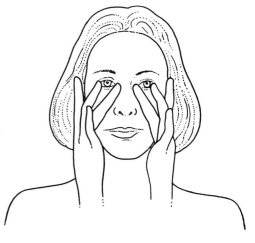

and around the eyes, and up towards the temple. Gently massage the temple area with circular movements, then slide the fingers back to the starting place. Repeat 5 times.

UNDER-EYE PUFFINESS
Slide the middle finger of your right hand up and down the centre of your nose several times. Using both hands then, from the sides of your nose and with small circular movements, move your fingertips outwards and upwards to your temples, to the count of one to eight (following your under-eye bone structure). Then slide your fingers back to the side of your nose, to the same count. Repeat 5 times.

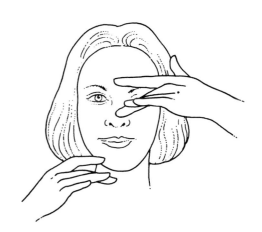

DROPPED LIPLINE AND LAUGHTER LINES
Create light, circular, upward and outward movements with your fingers at each side of the mouth, 5 times. Next, use the index finger of each hand to lightly lift the edges of your mouth, with quick, gentle movements, 5 times.

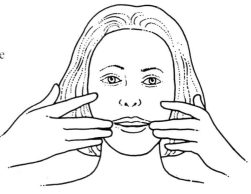

Face and neck exercises for flexibility

When driving your car, vacuuming the carpet, waiting for the kettle to boil or any other boring job you have to do, also practise the following face and neck exercises. Do the ones most relevant for you, and repeat them as many times as you feel comfortable with.

Strengthen muscles around the mouth   Purse your lips, then open your mouth and eyes as wide as possible.

Help lift a drooping lip line   Purse lips, then pull them into a broad smile.

Tone up and relax mouth, cheek and nose-to-mouth lines   Keeping teeth and lips closed, blow a ball of air under your upper lip; hold for a cound of 10. Then move it to the left side of your mouth; hold for 10. Then move it to the bottom lip area; hold for 10. Then move it to the right-hand side of your face; hold for 10. Relax. Repeat.

Relax and strengthen lip muscles   Hold teeth together, part your lips in a wide smile. Close lips and widen the eyes. Repeat.

Workout for eyelid muscles that helps to hold back crow's feet and works wonders on under-eye puffiness. Keeping your head still, look straight forward. Now look upward, then down – keeping head still. Then turn eyes to the right, then to the left. Repeat.

Help lift a double chin   Open your eyes wide, and purse your lips. Then try to bring lips and eyes towards one another. Then open eyes and mouth wide. Hold for a count of 10 at each stage. Relax for same count. Then repeat.

Relax tension and tone neck and shoulder muscles   Drop your chin on to your chest, then slowly move your chin round towards your left shoulder. Return to centre. Then move towards the right and back. Repeat 3–5 times each side. Carefully tilt your head back, as far as it will go comfortably, then forward. Repeat 3–5 times each way.

COLOUR CHARACTERISTICS

Each of these three girls has different colour characteristics. Look at the girls in turn and decide which of the following words best describes your first impression of them: light, dark, muted, bright, cool or warm. To find out whether you are right, turn to page 99 where you will also learn how to recognise your own colour characteristics.

Avis

Susan

Ann

THE 18 COLOUR FANS

Depending on your colour characteristics (see pages 97-104), certain shades and intensities of colours will suit you better than others. For example, if you are a Dark/muted you will be able to wear colours from the **Dark** fan and the **Dark muted** fan (see pages 144-150).

Dark Fan (From left to right) *True Red, Mahogany, Royal Purple, Dark Periwinkle Blue, True Blue, Teal Blue, Pine Green, Forest Green, Olive Green, Yellow Gold*

Dark Bright (From left to right) *Deep Hot Pink, Magenta, Shocking Pink, Bright Burgundy, Medium Violet, Royal Blue, Chinese Blue, True Green, Emerald Green, Bright Yellow*

Dark Muted (From left to right) *Pumpkin, Rust, Dark Tomato Red, Muted Purple, Marine Navy, Terracotta, Turquoise, Moss Green, Coffee Brown, Warm Beige*

Light Fan (From left to right) *Pastel Pink, Clear Salmon, Deep Rose, Water Melon Red, Medium Violet, Medium Blue, Powder Blue, Light Blue Green, Light Lemon Yellow, Light Blue Grey*

Light Muted (From left to right) *Powder Pink, Orchid, Mauve, Rose Pink, Rose Beige, Pastel Blue Green, Deep Blue Green, Pastel Aqua, Sky Blue, Grey Blue*

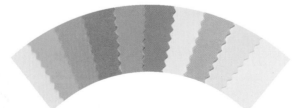

All colours are subject to the limitations of the printing process

Light Bright (From left to right) *Warm Pastel Pink, Coral Pink, Clear Bright Pink, Clear Bright Red, Golden Tan, Periwinkle Blue, Light Clear Gold, Light Aqua, Peach, Buff*

Bright Fan (From left to right) *Shocking Pink, Clear Bright Pink, True Red, Medium Violet, Deep Periwinkle Blue, True Blue, Chinese Blue, Hot Turquoise, True Green, Bright Yellow*

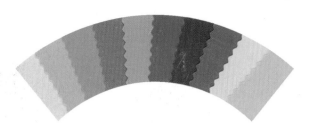

Bright Light (From left to right) *Peach, Clear Salmon, Bright Coral, Clear Bright Red, Emerald Turquoise, Light True Blue, Light Clear Navy, Clear Bright Aqua, Light Clear Gold, Light Warm Grey*

Bright Dark (From left to right) *Deep Hot Pink, Magenta, Blue Red, Bright Burgundy, Royal Purple, Royal Blue, Light True Green, Emerald Green, Lemon Yellow, Black*

Muted Fan (From left to right) *Deep Apricot, Watermelon Red, Muted Burgundy, Muted Purple, Grey Navy, Jade Green, Olive Green, Rose Brown, Green Grey, Gold*

Muted Dark (From left to right) *Salmon, Bittersweet, Warm Purple, Mahogany, Dark Chocolate Brown, Moss Green, Forest Green, Teal Blue, Autumn Grey, Camel*

Muted Light (From left to right) *Rose Pink, Mauve, Deep Rose, Light Periwinkle Blue, Medium Blue Grey, Deep Blue Green, Medium Blue Green, Light Lemon Yellow, Powder Blue, Light Blue Grey*

Warm Fan (From left to right) *Peach, Salmon, Bright Orange, Rust, Medium Golden Brown, Yellow Gold, Bright Yellow Green, Turquoise, Teal Blue, Warm Purple*

Warm Light (From left to right) *Light Apricot, Bright Coral, Orange, Orange Red, Light Clear Gold, Golden Tan, Clear Bright Aqua, Lime Green, Emerald Turquoise, Dark Periwinkle Blue*

Warm Dark (From left to right) *Pumpkin, Terracotta, Mahogany, Medium Bronze, Dark Chocolate Brown, Olive Green, Forest Green, Dark Periwinkle, Muted Purple, Dark Tomato Red*

Cool Fan (From left to right) *Fuchsia, Plum, Blue Red, Grey Navy, Grey Blue, Deep Blue Green, Emerald Green, Lemon Yellow, Rose Beige, Rose Brown*

Cool Light (From left to right) *Soft Burgundy, Soft Fuchsia, Orchid, Powder Pink, Lavender, Powder Blue, Medium Blue Green, Medium Blue Grey, Pastel Blue Green, Light Lemon Yellow*

Cool Dark (From left to right) *Shocking Pink, Magenta, True Red, Royal Purple, Bright Burgundy, Royal Blue, Charcoal Grey, True Green, Bright Yellow, Light True Grey*

CHAPTER SEVEN

Skin Colours for a Youthful You

Looking your best and most youthful means maximising your looks. Women can improve their appearance with the careful use of cosmetics. As well as being important to learn how to apply them properly, it's vital that you choose the best shades for your own particular colouring.

In this chapter we concentrate on showing you how to assess your colour characteristics and then how to use this knowledge to help you choose the most flattering make-up colours. In Chapters 8 and 12 you will find advice on choosing hair colouring and clothes to suit your personal colour characteristics.

YOUR COLOURING AND THE SIX CHARACTERISTICS OF COLOUR

One of the most important aspects of colouring is how skin, hair and eye colour interact with one another to give an overall picture. Let me give you some examples: If you have dark hair, by contrast your skin will always look lighter than it really is. Conversely, a medium to dark skin against light hair will always look muted.

Eyes also play their part. Indeed, the three interplay with one another to create your overall, unique looks.

Colour is three-dimensional. It has DENSITY, CLARITY and UNDERTONE. Each dimension can be classified in one of two ways, giving six characteristics of colour:

Density can be light or dark
Clarity can be muted or bright
Undertone can be cool or warm

Your colouring can be classified by assessing which of these six characteristics give the best overall description of you. Which do you see first? If your overriding impression is of light hair and eyes, for example, then 'Light' would be your first characteristic. Alternatively if your overriding impression is warm looking hair, skin and eyes, your first characteristic would be 'Warm'. Then try to assess which is your second dominant characteristic.

It may be helpful to look at the scales below and award a percentage score to your most dominant characteristics. The categories on pages 100–101 may help you, as well as the following examples.

COLOUR

Density Scale

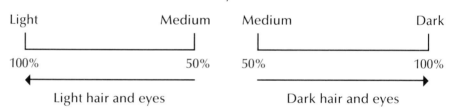

Clarity Scale

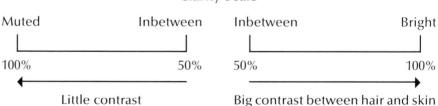

Undertone Scale

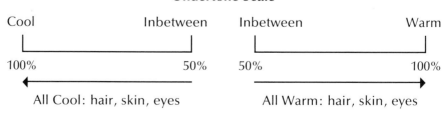

Three examples

Before we go any further let's practise by taking a look at three examples. First take a look at the photographs opposite page 96.

Avis, has dark hair, dark brown eyes and a medium to dark skin. Now consider the six characteristics of colour and pick one word from the six which gives the best overall description of Avis. 'Dark?' Yes, that's right; it is the best overall description. Avis gets 90% for density, in favour of the dark hair and eyes which make 'Dark' her first colour characteristic.

Her second characteristic gets 70% in favour of 'Muted' – created by her medium dark skin looking slightly muted against the dark background of her hair and eyes. (If Avis's skin had been medium light this would have given her a brighter skin look and that would have made her second characteristic 'Bright'.) This makes Avis a 'Dark muted'. Just because Avis has coloured skin doesn't automatically mean her first characteristic will be 'Dark'. If she had had a more blended look (if her skin, hair and eyes were closer together in intensity) she would be a 'Muted dark'.

Susan has dark hair, light skin and medium blue/green eyes creating strong contrast. Which overall word describes Susan best? 'Bright' is the best overall description and gets 80%. Her second characteristic gets 60% in favour of 'Dark'. (If Susan's eyes had been light this would have given her a lighter look and made her second characteristic 'Light'.) This makes Susan a 'Bright dark'.

Ann has medium-warm blonde hair, medium-warm eyes and light-warm skin. Which overall word describes Ann best? Yes, 'Warm'. This gets 100%. Her second characteristic is light close to medium and so gets 60% in favour of 'Light'. (If Ann's skin had been medium this would have given her a darker toned-down look and would have made her second characteristic 'Dark'.) This makes Ann a 'Warm light'.

Your colour characteristics

Now it's your turn. Pick a word from the six characteristics of colour which gives the best overall description of you. Now look to the remaining four characteristics to find your second dominant characteristic.

This method of self analysis is the easiest, most up-to-date and accurate but sometimes we find it difficult to be objective about ourselves. If this is your problem, you might find it easier first to eliminate what you are not. If you are still not sure, ask a friend or relative to help you. Remember you are judging whether your colouring gives an overall light, medium or dark intensity – taking your ethnic background into consideration.

Choosing make-up colours

Now you have discovered your natural colour characteristics of hair, skin and eyes, you can use this knowledge to help you choose your best make-up colours. These, correctly applied, can give a quick transformation, and take years off your looks. Once we turn 30 we should think of make-up differently to the way we did at 16, when we used it as a cover up, so we could look older. Now we need to use it to achieve a natural look, and to give our face a lift and make us look younger. Here's how:

Dark bright   Dark hair, dark eyes, fair skin = contrast.
Light natural foundation, medium blusher and bright to dark lipstick.

Dark muted   Dark hair, dark eyes, medium skin = subtle contrast.
Medium to dark beige foundation, medium muted blusher, dark to medium lipstick.

Light bright   Light to medium hair, medium bright eyes, light skin = light to medium contrast.
Light to medium ivory foundation, medium blusher, medium-bright lipstick.

Light muted   Light to medium hair, medium eyes, medium skin = very little contrast.
Light to medium pink-beige foundation, light muted blusher, medium muted lipstick.

Bright light   Dark to medium hair, light to medium eyes, fair skin = contrast.
Light to medium ivory foundation, medium blusher, bright light lipstick.

Bright dark   Dark hair, medium/deep eyes, fair skin = contrast.
Light to medium natural foundation, medium to deep blusher, bright to deep lipstick.

Muted light   Medium to light hair, medium eyes, medium skin = little contrast.
Light to medium pink-beige foundation, medium muted blusher, medium muted lipstick.

Muted dark   Medium to dark hair, medium to dark eyes, medium skin = very little contrast.

Deep ivory or beige foundation, medium muted blusher, medium to deep muted lipstick.

Warm light Medium hair, light/medium eyes, fair skin = contrast between the medium/bright.
Light to medium ivory foundation, medium warm blusher, bright warm lipstick.

Warm dark Medium to dark hair, medium to deep eyes, medium skin = subtle contrast.
Medium warm to deep beige foundation, medium warm blusher, medium to deep warm lipstick.

Cool light Medium hair, light to medium eyes, light to medium skin = medium contrast.
Light pink-beige foundation, medium to light blue-pink blusher, medium blue-pink/red lipstick.

Cool dark Medium to dark hair, medium to deep eyes, medium skin = medium to deep contrast.
Medium pink-beige foundation, medium blue-pink blusher, medium to deep blue-pink/red lipstick.

Lips Always look to your main colour characteristic as your first consideration when choosing a lipstick. For example, if the first characteristic is 'Warm', and the second 'Light', your best lipstick colour will be warm light reds, pinks and copper shades.

Finding the best shade of foundation

To select the best foundation for your skin colour, look for those which have the same intensity as your own skin. For example: light skin = light foundation.

You could find two or three foundations which have the right light intensity but have the wrong clarity or undertone. So the next step is to test one against the other. Consider light ivory vs light pink-beige or light grey-beige. Place a dot of each across the centre of your forehead, leave for a few seconds to allow the foundation to react to the body's natural acid, then spread the dots and slightly blend. The foundation which disappears, leaving a smooth looking skin surface, is the right one for you.

Those foundations that are still visible after spreading will age you, but you may find that a very slightly lighter foundation will lift the skin colour and tone and make you look younger.

Eye make-up colours

When using colours around the eyes, always remember that light brings forward and dark takes away (recedes), so:

- Apply lightest shades on the areas of the eye you want to bring forward or make larger

- Use darker shades on areas you want to push back

Any shade or intensity which takes attention away from your eyes is too strong.

A very light person will not look good in very dark eyeshadow once crêpiness or crow's feet start to show. A very dark person will look wrong in very light eyeshadow, except for a little used to give lift to the eyes. Use a magnifying glass to pick out your secondary and tertiary eye colours. Use your darker shades on the creases and outer lid, medium shades on the lids and lighter shades on the brow bone and inner lid.

Brown eyes can wear a wide variety of colours: lavender, mauve, peach, olive to brown. Let the intensity of your eyes guide you as to how light or dark you should go.

Hazel eyes may be blue hazel, green hazel, grey hazel, brown hazel. Their colour will change with the clothing worn, or the immediate environment. Pick out secondary and tertiary eye colours and use smokey shades of these to make eye colour stand out and control its change of colour.

Green eyes Warm green eyes need colours with a warm undertone: peach, copper, gold and turquoise. Cooler green eyes need muted mauve, lavender or blue grey.

Blue eyes Blue looks good when it is slightly muted and toned down. Bright blue and green shadows which take over are wrong. Blue eyes with yellow in them look good against aqua, peach, orange and bronze. Cooler looking blue eyes look good with greys, blue-grey, plum and lavender.

Spectacle wearers Apply a little more colour than normal so it can still be seen through the lenses.

The more you experiment with colours, the greater your confidence will grow. Try mixing leftover, rarely used eyeshadows together to make different colours. See how a bright blue mixed with bright orange turns into a muted, toned-down colour. Try other combinations on white paper and learn how to work with colour.

Face savers

The following will all help over-thirties to hold back the sighs:

- Blemish coverstick, to cover spots, scars, or birthmarks. Apply with your middle finger and blend the edges before applying foundation.

- Concealer minimises wrinkles, smile and frown lines and under-eye puffiness and evens out skin tone. Use a few dots of concealer on a fine brush or sponge. Use the same colour or slightly lighter than your natural skin colour and gently blend it in. Or use a green tinted one to cover red blotches and broken capillaries, stippling and gently blending. Use a purple one to correct sallow skin.

- A foundation which matches your skin tone or is one shade either side (never more) will even out your skin tone. A light textured foundation with the same intensity will always look more youthful. Apply foundation lightly all over the eye area.

- Loose translucent powder comes next, lightly applied. Brush downwards with a make-up brush to remove any excess, not forgetting in and around the eye area.

- Eyebrow pencil. If your eyebrows are light or sparse, use short feathery pencil strokes to make them look more natural and frame the eye: never go darker than the darkest shade in your hair – sometimes even this is too harsh.

- Mascara. All eyes look better when the lashes frame the eye. Make sure you brush the lashes well out to stop lumping and spiking. Use colours which complement your hair colour in intensity.

- Eyeliner should never be extended to the inside corner of your eye, unless you deliberately want to make your eyes look small and beady. Also, as we mature, it is not a good idea to wear black liner on the lower, inner lid. Always lightly smudge eyeliner to avoid harsh lines.

- Use less eyeshadow as you get older, and be aware of changing styles of eye make-up. Avoid bright colours, because they look artificial on an older face. Also avoid glittery, shiny eyeshadows as they show every crease. Eyeshadow should be well blended to emphasise your eyes, not the shadow. Matt will always look best on eyes beginning to lose their sparkle; avoid a high shine.

- If you use highlighter, choose matt. Apply to the upper edge of each cheekbone.

- Blusher should always be used subtly, to achieve a delicate, natural glow. Cream blusher looks more natural on an older face than powder blusher. Look straight ahead and find the point where the middle of the iris and the end of your nose would meet if you drew an imaginary line straight down from the iris and across from the nose. Apply a little dot of cream blusher with the fingertips here, and apply two more dots in a straight line going diagonally upwards and outwards. Blend upward and outward towards the ears, taking care not to blend higher than the cheek bone or top of the ear, and no lower than the ear lobes, which would make the face look less youthful. Blend until colour fades into the hairline. Brush a little under or over your outer brows.

- Lipliner (use a brush or pencil) helps as you grow older to define your lip shape and make the lipstick last longer and feather less. Lipliner should tone, or be slightly darker than your lipstick. Draw the outline of your lips, stopping short of the ends if your mouth is too wide or turns down.

- Lipstick colour should always be kept within your colour range. Example: Light/brights wear light bright lipsticks best.

- If your mouth has started to line, stick to matt lipsticks and don't put gloss on top.

- True reds make the teeth look whiter. If you can't wear bright reds go for coral shades instead.

For men only

Before male readers hurriedly turn the page, let us just say that most of the men admired for their handsome, rugged good looks – whether on film, television or in person – wear some form of skin corrector, camouflage or bronzing gel. Yes, there is an increasing readiness among men to enhance their appearance and practise a little illusion. Why not? You've been doing it with shoulder pads for many a year, and you can be in no doubt by now that sun bathing without protection can have a disastrous effect on your skin. So using a bronzer makes good sense.

If you have a light to medium skin colour, go lightly on the application. The secret is to squeeze just a little into your wet palms, rub your hands together and then spread quickly and evenly all over.

Bronzers come in many forms from tinted sports gels, to tinted moisturisers and tanning gels. They are waterproof, but easily removed with soap and water, so why not experiment a little and see what they can do for you.

· CHAPTER EIGHT ·

Hair: Our Crowning Glory

Your hair is, in fact, an extension of your skin and contains the same pigment cells. It also participates in the ageing process with the skin, both losing their pigment. However, the hair is easily coloured to visually cheat the hands of time, and many take this option.

HOW HAIR GROWS

Except for the palms, soles and mucous membranes, hair is found over the entire skin surface. There are two basic types of hair: the readily visible, coarse hair which is found on the scalp, beard, armpits and genital areas (and for some people, the arms, chest and legs), and the fine, soft, almost invisible hairs found elsewhere.

Hormones, the natural, regulatory substances your body produces, influence the hair. Among the many changes that occur at puberty, hormones cause the invisible hair under the arms, around the genitals and the beard area of men to become coarse, visible hair. Puberty also causes some changes to head hair. Later in life, changes in the balance of the same hormones cause many men to go bald in a consistent pattern called 'male-pattern baldness'.

A hair grows from a tube of cells that fold down, like an inverted balloon, from the epidermis, right into the dermis. This structure, appropriately called a hair follicle, forms a tube extending deep into the dermis. The hair follicle bulges out at its base into a bulb, commonly called the root. The hair grows from this root. Hair root cells go through a life cycle similar to skin cells. They reproduce at the bottom and migrate upwards; consequently, the hair grows up. But instead of producing a layer of dead, keratin cells as they do on the skin, these cells in the root produce the hair shaft.

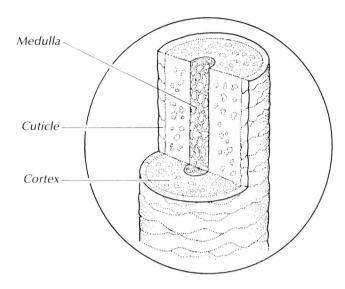

Medulla

Cuticle

Cortex

A hair shaft resembles a wire made of firmly packed 'dead' cells with a unique design. Except for the cells at the base, the hair is a dead structure. A thin, hard, glossy outer-coating, the **cuticle**, acts as a protective sheathe and gives the hair a sheen if the cuticle contains oil. Immediately beneath the cuticle is the **cortex**, which resembles the insulation around a strand of wire. The **medulla** is the actual core or wire – the centre of the hair.

Pigment cells, similar to those in the skin, also pack into the cortex and impart colour to the hair. Colour variation is created by the amount of pigment and air trapped between the packed cells that make up the cortex.

Phases of hair growth

An average head has about 100,000 hairs. Some hairs grow faster than others and hair grows somewhat differently for each person. Some people's hair lengthens by an inch in one month, while for others, an inch of growth takes three months.

Hair grows in cycles. About 90% of hair is in the active growing or **anagen** phase and the other 10% is in the resting, **telagen** stage.

The telagen phase lasts three to six months; then the hair goes into the anagen phase and starts growing. During the resting phase, the attachment between the hair and the shaft weakens and the hair falls out. So, with 100,000 hairs on a human head, it's normal for about 90 hairs to fall out daily. I emphasise normal because, under some conditions, many more fall out. Most of these hairs grow back. Obviously, if more fall out than grow back, you will gradually become bald. Unfortunately, once a hair follicle dies, it can't be resurrected.

Stress, illness and poor nutrition can cause thinning hair in both men and women. Good nutrition – sometimes more protein and vitamins – often helps return this situation to normal.

Most men and women lose some hair as they age. However, heredity plays a big role in hair loss in men and to a lesser degree in women. Therefore, if you suffer from unusual hair loss, see a dermatologist.

Maintaining healthy hair

Hair follicles extend deep into the dermis so they can benefit from its abundant supply of blood, with its nourishing oxygen and all the necessary nutrients. Consequently, healthy blood-circulation with correct nutrient-balance produces strong, healthy hair. If the root cells at the base of the follicle contain the correct oils and pigments, the hair will also contain them.

On the following table are listed steps you can take to nourish your hair follicles. Well-nourished hair follicles, more correctly well-nourished basal cells, produce healthy hair.

Healthy hair follicles

Improvers	Detractors
Aerobic exercise	Poor fitness
Stress fighters	High stress
High-protein, low-fat diet	High-fat diet
Regularity	Constipation
No chemical abuse	Chemical abuse
and	Smoking
Sensible moderation	Alcohol
	Stimulants

Let's go through each factor so you'll see each objective clearly.

- Improve circulation: Good circulation sends oxygen and nutrient laden blood to each hair follicle. Good circulation requires regular aerobic exercise and a balanced, low-fat, high-protein diet.

- Avoid stress: Stress reduces the circulation of blood to the body surface; that means the hair follicles don't get their share. If you can't avoid stress, take extra protein, B vitamins and vitamin C to maintain good circulation.

- A high-fat diet and excessive body-weight also reduces peripheral circulation.

- Protein, in contrast to fat, improves hair growth. A high-protein, low-fat meal with complex carbohydrates alters your energy balance and generates internal body heat. This heat is dissipated by increasing circulation to the head and hands. Increased circulation improves the nutrient content delivered to each hair follicle. The result: a thicker, more dense hair.

- Regularity reduces your toxic burden; these toxins affect each hair-follicle.

- Chemical abuse: Any chemical abuse (including excess coffee, tea and alcohol) reduces nourishment flow to the hair follicle. The best defence is a good diet, regular exercise, no smoking and sensible supplementation.

Improving hair through diet

You can improve the growth and appearance of your hair through diet if you have patience; it will take at least three months before you begin to notice a change. However, you will have this crowning glory for life, so you might as well do everything you can to make it represent you as well as possible. I've summaried these steps in the table below.

Promoting healthy hair growth

Promoter	Result
Protein supplement ¾ oz (15–20 g)	Improved circulation and stronger hair
Fish and vegetable oil	Increased sheen and smoother cuticles
Vitamin/mineral supplementation	Optimum nutrients and better colour
Beta-carotene supplement	Improved colour and sheen

Oils in the basal cells are incorporated into each hair. That is oils, not fat. Eat fish regularly and take a marine-oil supplement when necessary. If your hair and skin seem dull, eat fish and take a marine-oil supplement, such as EPA or pure cod-liver oil. Follow the Longevity Diet and the sensible supplement plan in Chapter 2.

A daily protein supplement will improve peripheral circulation and the nourishment of each hair. Use the supplement at least 30 minutes before eating. This addition of about ¾ oz (15 g) of protein increases blood amino-acid levels and improves circulation to the hair follicles and finger nails so their growth and strength improves; you will see an improvement in about a month.

Beta-carotene improves hair and skin colour and especially the sheen of your hair.

External ageing factors

Diet affects the condition of your hair from the inside. But there are many external factors that can have an ageing effect too.

The sun attacks our hair with ultra-violet light waves which break down nutrients in the hair structure, making the cuticles wither and grow old, and leaving them unable to reflect light. This can make coarse grey hair even coarser. Sunshine also fades hair; it bleaches out some of the colour pigment. It can turn grey hair an unattractive and unnatural light yellow, fade dark hair, change the colour of colour treated hair, and make bleached hair look like straw. The same problems arise from too many permanents, too much bleaching, over-use of heated rollers and the wrong shampoo. Even vigorously towel-drying hair can break the ends. The sun isn't the only element that can damage and age our hair. Too much wind and cold weather will have the same effect, so always protect your hair from the elements. Chlorine from swimming pools can also have a disastrous effect on hair, so always wear a cap or a protective conditioner before going swimming.

CONDITION, COLOUR AND STYLE

Hair can be your crowning glory, or the bane of your life. Its condition, style and colour can affect not only how you look but also how you feel. It is potentially one of the most beautiful accessories you can have, and one of the most versatile. It can help you play whatever role your life demands of you with greater effectiveness and ease. So as well as putting into practice all the dietary recommendations given in this book, it is worth spending time finding a good hairstylist. You also need to learn which styles will suit your face shape.

KNOW YOUR FACE SHAPE

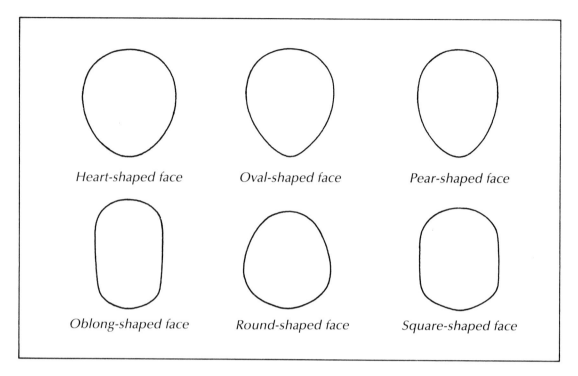

Heart-shaped face   Oval-shaped face   Pear-shaped face

Oblong-shaped face   Round-shaped face   Square-shaped face

The diagrams will help you to discover your face shape. Read on to discover which hair styles suit individual face shapes best.

Also, take into consideration your figure type and height. Judging a hairstyle is rather like buying a hat; you should always view yourself in a full length mirror so you can see whether it is balanced and in keeping with your overall look.

Lifestyle is the other main consideration. If you are a busy business woman, you need a simple but well cut hairstyle to suit your face and figure type, and which helps you project a neat, controlled look. Similarly, a mother or nanny who is always on the go supervising children would find a hairstyle that needs a lot of attention impossible to cope with. Also, if you can't afford to visit a hairdresser weekly, then it is obviously important to have a style that you can easily maintain between visits.

Women

Round shape

You need to create the illusion of length. Height will be needed at the crown and fullness above the eyes, with hair tapered towards the cheeks to minimise their width. A side parting with a small section of a fringe brought on to the forehead, asymmetrically, and the rest of the fringe raised up over the forehead will draw the eye up diagonally and lengthen the face. Hair worn very straight to below the chin, with an upward and outward style on top of the crown will give height. Avoid making the cheek area look broader.

Heart shape

You need to add width to the jawline, or visually narrow your forehead. Hairstyles that fall long and loose, and end at the jawline, will add width. Avoid showing all your forehead. Also avoid very short styles which add volume to the top half of your head area, heavy and very straight fringes or those that add width to your forehead.

Oval shape

This face shape can take a huge variety of hairstyles, but as you get older remember to go for a soft non-severe style.

Oblong shape

Add fullness to the sides and minimise the height. Long hair needs shaping well and should be shorter and fuller at the sides. Add width at the temples with wispy and full fringes cut deep into the sides of the hair. Shorter hair parted off-centre and fringes brushed to one side, or fullness through layering or perming will give needed horizonal fullness at check level.

Avoid a centre parting or hair high on top of the crown, very short cropped styles, hair combed straight back off the forehead, or straight hair styles.

Pear shape

You need to make the face look longer and narrower, to take the eye from the jawline: hair sweeping upwards in asymmetrical broken or layered lines looks best. Medium length hair with height at the top will lengthen your face; so will straight hair curved in at the jawline, short hair with sides swept back and height at the crown, hair parted off-centre, and loose, curly styles.

Square shape

To give visual balance you need to make the face look longer and narrower. Hair sweeping upwards in asymmetrical, broken lines looks best. Medium length hair with height at the top will lengthen your face; so will straight hair

curved in at the jawline, and short hair with sides swept back and height at the crown. Curly styles soften the angles of this face shape.

Avoid fullness at the jawline and exposing all the forehead, chin-length cuts, straight fringes or a centre parting which all add to the squareness.

Men

Round shape

Have your hair cut to give height on top and smooth sleek sides. A style brushed back from the forehead with a side or off-centre parting will give a slender line. Sideburns should not come lower than the middle of the ear.

Heart shape

Clip your hair shorter on the top and the sides. Keep the length at the back. Sideburns should not be too short.

Oval shape

You can wear most hair styles. Let your hairstylist help you choose one to suit your lifestyle and personality.

Oblong shape

This shape needs side fullness. Sideburns with a squarish look will add width.

Pear shape

This shape needs fullness adding to the top and sides to broaden the forehead. An off-centre parting and sideburns no lower than the middle of the ear will direct the eye upward and away from the jawline.

Square shape

Have a style which gives width and height; or a short all round cut to lengthen your face. Ask the stylist to angle your sideburns.

Choosing a style

Your hairstyle can make you look years younger – or older. It is all too tempting to stay with a style that suited you five, 10 or even 15 years ago, but nothing gives you a more dated look. Notice how Cher and Joan Collins (opposite) have changed with the times. To look younger, you must have a today's hairstyle – not way out but healthy, timeless and 'with it'. For men there are very good alternatives to the short back and sides without having to look as though you just stepped off a fashion page.

There are several major considerations when choosing a hairstyle: your lifestyle, your face shape, the type of hair you have, and its condition.

Knowing your face shape and what the basic styles will and will not do for it, then taking into consideration tips which will direct attention away from your not-so-good points, will help you to choose a flattering style.

Find one which also makes the most of your type of hair. Is your hair thinning? Is it fine and fly away? Thick and wiry, or strong and curly? Mother Nature very rarely gets it wrong, so if you have curly hair, first try to find a style which will make full use of it *and* enhance your looks. If, however, this is not what would make you feel good about yourself, there are straightening techniques available. Your hairstylist is the best one to advise you if your hair is suitable for straightening or, indeed, perming, as these treatments alter the basic structure of your hair and how it will look in relation to your face shape.

Once you have decided on a possible hairstyle, it's worth asking your hairdresser the following questions:

- What can you do to improve the condition and colour of your hair?

- Will your chosen style be suitable for your hair type?

- Will your chosen style suit the shape of your face?

- How difficult will it be to look after? Will it necessitate going back to the stylist more often than you have time for, or can you easily manage it yourself?

(continued on page 113)

STAY YOUNG AND ATTRACTIVE

People whose looks are their livelihood, for example fimstars and models, know they have to look good at all times. They are often masters of maintaining an ever-youthful image.

Take Joan Collins and Cher (below). Would you have guessed that there is a gap of 35 years between the two photographs of Joan Collins and about 22 years between the two photographs of Cher?

Joan Collins in 1955 (left) and in 1988 (right), looking as good as ever. She was born in 1933.

Cher in 1965 (left) and in 1987 (right). Cher was born in 1946. Notice how she has changed with the times. The long straight hair that was so fashionable in the sixties would look very dated on her now. It would also be very ageing and drag her features down.

A CHANGE FOR THE BETTER

You don't have to be a movie star to always look good. Follow the advice in this book and you will be a star in your own right. And don't forget that a change of hairstyle, make-up or the colours you wear can instantly make you look younger and more attractive.

Sally's colouring is light with a leaning towards bright. In the first picture (above left) Sally is wearing a black top which is too dark and ageing for her. It has the effect of pulling her face down and separating her head from her body.

In the second picture (above) Sally is wearing light bright colours which are in perfect harmony with her natural colouring. Light bright blusher and bright lipstick were used to enhance Sally's natural colouring and translucent skin. Sally's fine hair was cut with a sloping line to frame her face softly and emphasise her cheekbones. Soft golds, honey and apricot were used to colour and lighten the hair which complement Sally's complexion. Overall Sally has a younger fresher look which she loves.

The final picture (left) illustrates how Sally can wear colours from her light colour fan for a sophisticated business look.

Make-up by John Gustafson for Prescriptives
Hair by Billi Currie at Vidal Sassoon

Ann's colouring is dark with a slight leaning towards bright. She is a UK size 18 (USA 16) and her figure shape is ellipse.

In the picture above, Ann is wearing dark navy and white together in a straight style, making her look very stern and heavy.

Below, Ann is wearing a grey suit with a medium tan blouse which give her a very classy look without being overpowering. Ann's hair was restyled to give her a more sophisticated but easier to manage style which slims her face and makes her look younger. A chestnut brown conditioning rinse was applied to enhance Anne's natural colour and give more shine.

In the main picture Ann models a two-piece based on teal blue from her dark colour fan. It's flattering cut and soft neckline make her look slimmer and give her a go-anywhere look. Ann is delighted with the effect.

KEEPING UP APPEARANCES

Another example of someone familiar who looks as good now as he did over 20 years ago is Robert Redford. The first picture was taken in 1967, the second in 1988. In both he radiates health and vitality. He was born in 1936.

The second picture also shows that glasses do not have to be ageing. Chosen carefully to suit your face shape and colouring, they can actually be flattering. For more details see pages 121-125.

No doubt Robert Redford, like everybody else, has to work hard to maintain his image. It is seeing people like him that makes you realise that the effort and self-discipline required really are worthwhile.

We may not all have been born with the kind of filmstar looks of Joan Collins, Cher and Robert Redford but we can make the most of what we do have by looking after ourselves, caring about our appearance, and presenting the best possible immage at all times. And who doesn't want to look *and* feel younger and better?

Changing your hair colour

One of the changes which make us look older is when our hair turns grey. This is quite common in women and men in their thirties; some even show signs in their twenties. The solution is to use colourants to cover up those tell tale signs of age. They can also add shine and thickness. However, it's very important to have your facial hair tinted to match or blend with your head hair, so eyebrows and eyelashes don't look odd.

All colour changes first need serious consideration. Never change your hair colour on impulse. For instance going blonde – particularly if you are a natural brunette – is *not* your best look. Many women have quickly realised that, in fact, it gives their skin a very grey, ageing look. When you are past 30, colouring your hair darker than its natural colour makes more noticable any facial lines and adds years to your age.

Dark bright   Will always look best with dark hair. Any grey is best covered up, at least until totally grey; then it can look very attractive. If you fancy high or low lights, choose burgundy-subtle red or very slightly brown highlights or a brunette shade just a little lighter than your natural colouring.

Totally grey and you want to be blonde? Light to light-golden-blonde is best for you.

Dark muted   Will always look best with dark hair – and all the grey covered up. Use dark brunette shades (a shade lighter than your natural hair). If you fancy high or low lights, choose from medium brown, mahogany and bronze.

Light bright   Need to keep the brightness, and cover up all grey. Go for pale blonde, light to medium brown, even auburn. Remember, if over 30, always go lighter. Then natural, fine high-lighting helps you to brighten up dull looking hair.

Totally white/grey and you want to be blonde? A mix of light ash to light golden blonde is best.

Light muted   This is one head of hair where the grey nearly always looks good, mingled with the natural colour. If you decide to cover up the grey, be careful not to go too bright.

Totally white/grey and you want a blonde look? Go for a mix of deeper beiges and the ash shades.

Bright light   Need to keep some level of contrast from the skin, and hair going grey is more ageing to you. If covering grey, go for lighter than natural colour. Add some highlights if your hair is just looking dull.

Totally white/grey and you want to be blonde? Go for light to golden blonde or a mix.

Bright dark   Should maintain a strong level of contrast, with low lights of burgundy-subtle red or slightly lighter brown than the main hair colouring.

Totally white/grey and you want a blonde look? Light blonde to silvery white are best.

Muted light   Grey blends well with existing hair colour. If you want to cover the grey, take care not to go too bright.

Totally white/grey and you want a blonde look? Ash blonde is for you.

Muted dark   Looks best in a two or three tone effect of auburn, mahogany and/or warm brown.

Totally grey and you want a lighter look? The colours above mix well with grey. If you prefer to go blonde, go for a blend of medium and dark blonde and avoid blue rinses and too bright a blonde look.

Warm light   Should always maintain a warm, medium to light look and cover up all grey. This is best done by a two or three tone effect – traces of warm blonde with red, mahogany or warm brown.

Totally white/grey and you want a blonde look? Warm light golden blonde or a slight ivory white looks best.

Warm dark   Looks best when all grey is covered by a two or three tone effect: auburn, mahogany, warm brown or a little red.

Totally white/grey and you want a blonde look? Go for a mix of warm and medium beige.

Cool light   Looks good with grey hair once it is all grey. In the meantime you might prefer a toned-down ash-brown or ash blonde shade.

Totally white/grey and you want a blonde look? Go for silvery blonde or a hint of blue in your white.

Cool dark   Looks good with grey hair once it is all grey. In the meantime you might prefer a toned down ash brown shade.

Totally white/grey and you want a blonde shade? Go for light to medium ash blonde, or a hint of blue if you have a pink-toned skin. Greying or dull light to medium blonde or brown hair can get a tremendous boost from highlighting and streaking. Never go blonde if you have an olive skin.

Colour treatments at home

Because natural hair colour is closely related to skin tones, artifical colouring must be compatible with your complexion. In general, hair that is one or two shades lighter than the natural colour is most flattering when you are over 30, and it is best to start with a rinse that washes out. This type includes those products labelled 'rinses' and 'semi-permanent'.

A temporary rinse will make the biggest impact on naturally light to medium hair. You can enjoy using rinses to highlight, deepen, tone down, add reddish, bluish or golden tones to fading or grey hair.

Natural medium to dark heads of hair can expect a rinse to add brightness rather than colour, with the exception of a red rinse which leaves a touch of red. Temporary rinses coat the hair shaft and do not penetrate it; they can also add light, lustre and a hint of texture. They are often used as temporary toners for hair that is bleached, and needs extra tinting or toning down.

The semi permanents These 'four to six' week rinses are colour 'revivers' or hair 'brighteners', and give a more intense effect. They can't lighten colour, but they can brighten it, darken or blend in grey far better than mere rinses.

The permanents can't be washed out. Your hair colour will be 'permanently' changed and has to be constantly maintained if you want the new colour to look good; new growth will have your natural pigmentation, so regular root touching-up will be necessary.

Facial hair grooming for men

Eyebrows Your eyebrows are important because they frame the eyes, and if your 'frames' are looking grey or shaggy they will not enhance your eyes as they ought to. They should make you look youthful and alert, and enlarge the eye area. So ask your hairstylist or barber to trim them regularly.

Moustaches and beards Men can use facial hair to help shape their face. For example, a moustache which gently turns up at the ends will give a slight lift to the face. To keep your moustache well groomed use a styling grease which is sold in colours such as natural, blonde, chestnut, brown or black. The colour isn't permanent but it is water resistant.

A full beard will give width, while one which seems to just drop off the end of the face will give length, but whatever type you sport, make sure it always looks well trimmed. Bear in mind that in most cases facial hair can and does make men look older.

Unwanted facial hair is very ageing and gives you an unkempt look. One of the most effective ways of removing it (other than shaving) is waxing. This is inexpensive, whether you do it at home or have it professionally done in a salon, lasts three to four weeks and leaves the skin feeling soft.

A few stray hairs around the eyebrows, the corner of the mouth or growing out of your ears are best plucked. An ice cube pressed on the area to be plucked for a few seconds will make this painless. Use a good pair of tweezers and pluck the way the hair is growing.

Hairs protruding from nostrils may be cut or removed by electrolysis. Electrolysis is the only permanent means of hair removal, but it is slow and meticulous. Even then, the hair can be so strong that the needle only weakens it, so regrowth will occur and the process will have to be done again. However, with each treatment the hair follicle will weaken and finally give up the struggle.

Hair loss

This is becoming very common in men and women over 35, with some showing signs in their mid twenties. There are many possible causes for this: shock, anaemia, iron-deficiency, hyperactive or under active thyroid, infection with high fever, surgery, drug side-effects, crash dieting or a poor diet and stress. Fortunately, loss of hair due to these situations can be reversed by improving your diet and taking exercise (see Chapters 2 and 4).

Thinning hair
Special hair products and salon treatments can make your hair look thicker while you wait for the results of your improved diet. The chemical processes of colouring hair can add volume, as can a good cut or a root perm which will give lift and fullness. Remember though that you should still choose a style that suits your face shape. Thinning hair can look fuller if you keep it short.

Baldness
The most common form of hair loss is male pattern baldness. This usually occurs over a long period and there seems to be a consistent pattern. Gradual loss starts in the early twenties, accumulating in a great deal of hair loss at the front and centre of the scalp by the middle or late thirties. When this happens there is no sure way to encourage new hair growth, but massaging

to improve circulation to the hair follicles and stimulate their metabolism can be effective if done regularly.

Massage by cupping your scalp in your hands, using your thumbs as anchors and the tops of your fingers to rotate small areas of scalp. Never rub your scalp – simply rotate it as described, counting up to 25 before moving to a new spot. Continue in this way until the whole of the scalp has been covered. This should take just a few minutes a day.

For men who are going bald it is far better to have your existing hair well cut and styled to suit your face shape rather than growing bits of it long and sweeping them into odd positions in an attempt to disguise the bald patch. This only draws attention to the hair loss and ages you even more.

Many women find bald men particularly attractive and going bald is nothing to be ashamed of, nor should you feel the need to hide it. If, however, you want to cover it up, you could buy a hairpiece or full wig. Make sure it is the same colour as your hair and in a similar style, but don't wear a full wig all the time, as your scalp and hair need fresh air. With a hairpiece and a little practice, you can achieve a wide range of styles as well as effectively hide a problem area.

Hair transplant and implants   Transplants seem to be the most effective way of overcoming male pattern baldness, if you really can't learn to live with it. This surgical operation gives permanent results, once the transplanted hair has taken. It involves skin grafting and is done by taking ten hair follicles at a time from an area of the scalp where there is plenty of hair, and transplanting them to an area where hair is sparse. The newly transplanted hair falls out after approximately three months, but new hair will begin to grow in its place.

The operation is done under local anaesthetic, and between four and 16 sessions may be necessary, depending upon whether you just need to fill in a receding hairline or cover a large bald patch.

The most promising alternative treatment is **flap rotation**. This is carried out by a plastic surgeon, who removes flaps with an average of 10,000 hairs from the side of the head and replaces them on the front hair line. It usually requires two operations, carried out under local anaesthetic. This gives a quick natural appearance without the hair loss and time lag for re-growth which you experience with hair transplants.

By far the most exciting and interesting of the new ways of dealing with male-pattern baldness is that of using high-level nutritional supplementations, specifically high in anti-oxidant nutrients. This approach aims to rejuvenate and re-stimulate the failing glands and metabolic rate with diet, exercise and holistic health. This approach has got to be the best.

CHAPTER NINE

Eyes Right, Eyes Bright

Sight is the most dominant and important of all the senses, because it gives the brain over twice as much information as all the other senses combined. Sight is so overpowering that, when listening to good music, we automatically close our eyes to reduce the amount of information we feed our brain, in order that we can hear more keenly.

Vision is more complex than sight. It is what the brain 'sees', based on information and experience. For example, hold your fist at arm's length and it blocks out an object just across the street, such as a car, that is actually much larger. Your brain automatically interprets the information and you *know* your fist isn't bigger than the car. Vision is so overwhelming that we use it to tell someone how well we understand a concept; we say, 'I see'! The eye and brain are indeed intimately connected.

Eye/brain anatomy

Your eye is shaped like a ball. The term 'eyeball' is descriptive; it is like a very special camera enclosed within a clear, protein window, the cornea, that we see through. When you look in the mirror, you can barely see the cornea, as it is so clear and clean. The dark spot at the centre of your eye is actually an opening that lets light strike the lens just behind it. The coloured iris surrounding the opening, opens and closes to let just the correct amount of light through. The lens brings the light to a focus on the back of the eyeball, the retina. The retina is the most sensitive of all body tissues.

Eye colour resides in the iris and has the same origins as skin colour. People from northern origins have light, usually blue eyes because of lower light levels; as you approach equatorial origins, the eye colours become more and more black.

Your eye lens can focus instantly on this page, the house across the street, a plane in the sky and a star 1,000,000 light years away. You can do this because the brain focuses the lens on what you want to see. Unlike a glass lens, the lens in your eye is focused by muscles within your eyeball, at the edge of the lens, that change its shape. No man-made lens can change focus so quickly and smoothly.

Nearsighted, farsighted, or astigmatic?

You have probably taken the Snellen eye-test in school or at a doctor's clinic. You read a chart on a wall about 20 ft (6 m) away, with an enormous E at the top. This chart was devised by Dr. Herman Snellen in Holland over 150 years ago, to reveal abnormalities in sight, which can usually be corrected with glasses.

If you can't read the Snellen test correctly, it is usually because your eye is not correctly shaped. The focused image might fall in front of your retina producing nearsightedness or myopia; this means you can focus on things close, but need corrective lenses for distant objects. If the image focuses behind the retina, you're farsighted, (hyperopia), and need glasses for close work. A variation is when you see the images partly correct; that is astigmatism, or twisted vision. These problems can be easily corrected with glasses. See pages 122–124 for how to choose spectacle frames to suit your face shape and your colouring.

Ageing causes our eyes to change in several ways and we often require glasses as we get older. The most common change is an inability to focus easily on near objects. Hence, many of us require reading glasses. This happens because our lenses lose some flexibility and can't adjust as well and our eyeballs actually become somewhat elongated.

These minor changes can work in our favour, because some people who needed glasses for distant vision find they can get along with either a milder correction or no correction at all.

However, the need for glasses is nothing to be worried about. It is the same slowing down of the body that keeps us from running as fast or swimming as far as we always did. But it is important to get correct nourishment so our eyes do not lose their visual sensitivity and to prevent, as much as possible, cataracts.

A window to your health   As part of a physical examination, the doctor may ask you to look at some distant object while he looks around inside your eyeball with a small light. He's studying the state of your cornea and retina, the clarity of your lens, and the blood vessels that bathe your eye. In studying the first three, he is trying to detect early problems and prevent them from getting worse. When looking at the fine blood vessels, he's actually looking inside your body, to get an idea about the state of your circulation and to see if your blood is a bright red. If both eyes are not the same, there is a circulatory problem. The doctor can even get a feeling for blood content. For example, sometimes blood fats are so high these small vessels are not red, but milky looking. The doctor can see if there is high blood pressure or diabetes. Your eyes are literally a window to your health.

Eye tests   Two types of doctors concern themselves with sight and the eyes: an optometrist and an ophthalmologist respectively. An optometrist is not usually a medical doctor but he is trained to identify sight problems such as near-sightedness, and analyses sight for corrective glasses. He can also detect other problems for which the ophthalmologist is required. The ophthalmologist is a medical doctor who deals with medical conditions. Your eyes should be checked bi-annually by an optometrist; if he or she spots something besides the need for a sight correction, you will then be referred to an ophthalmologist.

Nutrition and eye health

Mother's milk contains everything an infant needs to thrive, and since 1975, two of its nutrients have been identified as essential for correct eye development: taurine, an unusual sulphur-amino-acid, and DHA, an abbreviation for docosahexaneoic acid. The mother makes all the necessary taurine from a good diet with high-quality protein.

DHA is an omega-3 oil you can get in limited amounts from green vegetables, but is most plentiful in cold-water fish. Follow the Longevity Diet, or take the fish-oil supplements discussed in Chapter 2 to ensure you are getting enough DHA.

In the ancient world, Arabs used carrots to improve or restore night vision. Later, in 450 B.C., Hippocrates used calves' liver. His cure was faster because calves' liver already contains vitamin A, and night vision would return within 24 hours. Carrots supply beta-carotene which our body must then convert to vitamin A, so night vision returns more slowly.

This story illustrates how sensitive our eyes are to nutrients and I can add that all the other nutrients are essential for good sight and vision. Follow the Longevity Diet and you will do fine. Over 20% of people who have a problem with night vision prove not to have enough beta-carotene or vitamin A in their diet.

Our eyes aren't quite as sensitive to other nutrients as they are to vitamin A, but a brief review of the most important ones is worthwhile.

- Vitamin C is critical in all tissues, but the eye lens is especially rich in vitamin C. This means that the lens will be susceptible to anything that robs the body of vitamin C.

- The B vitamins, especially B_{12}, seem to be involved in focusing and visual sensitivity. This isn't surprising, because these functions require energy. After all, focusing is accomplished with muscles and image transmission is an energy-requiring process. All energy production in the body requires the B vitamins.

- A lack of zinc and chromium has been strongly implicated in a number of visual problems. They bring to the fore the need for a balanced and varied diet; especially including meat, fish, grains and beans.

- Vitamins A, E, and K, are fat-soluble vitamins and are essential for good vision, but also for protection of the eye tissues. Actually, beta-carotene is better than vitamin A because it is used to make vitamin A and is a protector itself.

- It is also important to drink lots of water. Your eyes are constantly bathed with fluid we call tears, but dehydration reduces all body fluids, including tears. Tears contain enzymes to kill bacteria, and help get rid of some chemical pollution that reaches the eyes. But most of all, they are a continual bath for our eyes; they keep them clean, clear and germ free.

Irritants

Eyes are even more sensitive to irritants than our skin. When irritated, they often swell or become bloodshot. Bloodshot eyes are a common response to excess alcohol or minor irritants and they usually clear up in a day or two. However, if the eyes swell or bloodshot eyes persist, don't take any chances; see an eye doctor.

GLASSES

These days, both men and women are wearing glasses whether or not they actually need them to improve their vision, because glasses are now often used to make a fashion statement. Frames, however, should be chosen to suit the wearer, rather than for fashion alone. Ask yourself: Do the frames suit your face shape? Do they fit comfortably? Does the colour harmonise with your skin, hair and eye colour? Those that suit you and are in harmony with the rest of you will add to your appearance rather than detracting from it and ageing you.

CHOOSING GLASSES

Face shapes

Generally speaking, square and round faces are almost as broad as they are long; oblong shapes are visibly longer, while heart shapes go from wide to narrow. Oval shapes are ideally balanced. Depending on your face shape, here's what to look for:

Square shape

Off-straight horizontal lines will create width at the top, with a light frame or frameless bottom edge which could have a downward sweep to create more angles. Slightly curved frames with a little height on top are also ideal.

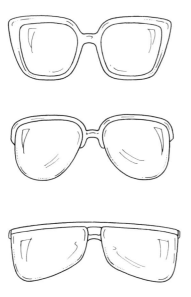

Round shape

Needs frames with straight sides, to create a sleek, more slender look (don't go for a square shape); alternatively, the frames could be straight across the top.

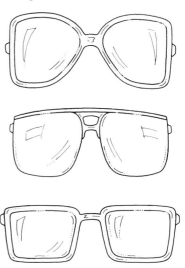

Oblong shape

Usually needs frames with definite horizontal lines top and bottom, to give some width and visual broadening.

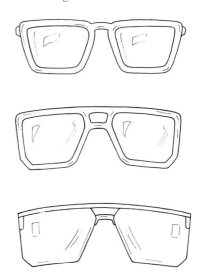

Heart shape

Needs to balance up a broad forehead and narrow jawline. A down-swept frame with outer dominant vertical lines will accentuate the lower half of the face.

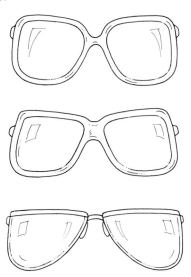

Pear shape

Select frames with a broad horizontal line at the top, and little or no heaviness to the rest of the frame.

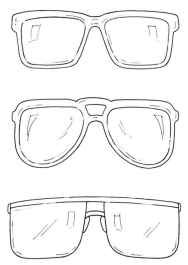

Oval shape

Is more balanced, so there is a much wider choice of suitable frames.

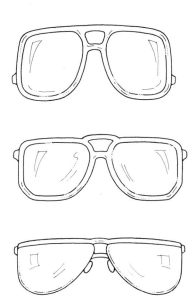

Trying on glasses

Comfort Look for a style where the bridge rests comfortably on your nose, without pinching and does not emphasise any facial lines.

Coloured lenses These can reflect on your skin; make sure that the reflection is in harmony with your skin tone (see Chapter 7). Avoid yellow tints which are generally more ageing.

Profile and nose shape Just as the length of your eyebrows can affect the apparent length of your nose, so can the bridge of your spectacles. The keyhole bridge sits high up the nose and makes a short nose look longer, while the saddle bridge has a shortening effect. The side arms, too, can reduce or lengthen the profile, so use two mirrors when trying on. Examine and try a broad arm and then a thin, narrow one; note the difference each makes to your profile.

Colour, materials and weight

Your skin, hair and eye colouring are the keys to choosing the colour of frame that will be most flattering to you.

Women who prefer a light or softer look can opt for pastel, or two-tone styles, or bright colours for a more trendy or sporty appearance. For a career woman, a more authoritative look can be achieved by light to dark neutrals, or heavier looking frames such as tortoiseshell, or lighter, metal frames.

Men are best advised to avoid pastels or trendy colours, unless in one of the creative arts, such as the theatre, television or advertising, or when you want a more relaxed look, in keeping with leisurewear. The more classic or neutral colours, or metals (which doesn't mean they have to be boring), are the ones to go for.

Warm, Bright and **Dark** If any of these are your first colour characteristic, gold metals look best.

All Cools, and **Light/muted** and **Muted/light** wear slightly toned down silver metals best.

Dark/muted, Muted/dark and **Warm/dark** wear coppery and bronze metals best.

Wearing glasses for short-sightedness

If you wear glasses because you are short sighted, the lenses will probably be thinner in the centre and thicker at the edges. This gives the effect of rounding out the eye and making it look smaller. You can lessen this effect by choosing a thinner frame which will offset the thickness of the lens, and by selecting non-reflective lenses as these are less apparent and make it easier for others to focus on your eyes instead of your spectacles. Eye make-up can also be used to open up the eyes and make them look larger (see page 102).

Wearing glasses for long-sightedness

Wearing glasses because you are long sighted usually means that your lenses are thick in the centre and thinner at the edges. Such lenses tend to make the eyes look larger as well as any lines around your eyes. Coloured or tinted lenses can help here, but avoid yellow tints, which are generally more ageing, and make sure the colour is in harmony with your skin tone. Alternatively, concealer can be used to cover up crow's feet, and careful use of eye make-up can tone down the dilated look which long-sighted lenses can project.

Non-reflective lenses

If you wear spectacles and have problems with reflections, either through eye strain or the glare caused by car headlights, watching television or working under artifical lights, non-reflective lenses could be the answer.

CHAPTER TEN

Hands, Feet, Nails and Teeth

NAILS

The healthy condition of our nails, like the rest of our body, depends on good circulation and balanced nutrition, but fingernails go one step further – they let us see our circulation at work. Look directly down at a fingernail and what you see is the nail plate. The base of the nail, where it disappears into the finger, is the cuticle. Beneath that is the nail bed, which attaches the nail plate to the finger. Nail growth takes place in the cuticle and its health is influenced in the nail bed. At the base of the nail is a white, half-moon area, called a lunula. This is where the protein keratin comes from that forms the matrix of the nail. The area past the lunula, beneath the nail, is the nail bed (the dermis). The pinkish colour of the nail bed comes from the many small blood-vessels of capillaries it contains.

The nail is dead, keratinised tissue – mostly protein. The nails are firmly attached to the nail bed and the cuticle from which it grows. A nail grows from the cuticle out and takes about four to eight months to be complete (nails grow only about ⅛ of an inch/3 mm a month).

Ridges and lines   As you examine your nail plate, you will notice ridge lines extending from the cuticle to the tip. These lines are the result of growth patterns that are characteristic of the cuticle; like finger prints, your nail ridges are not exactly the same as anyone else's. Ridge lines can be changed however. For example, if you damage the cuticle, a new line may develop, and it will be with you always. Ridge lines also change as we get older.

Splitting nails   Most people, especially women, complain that their nails crack and split. These complaints seem to start at about the age of 25 and reach a maximum between age 35 and 45, then remain stable. Since we know that nail growth is related to circulation, it is also influenced by nutrition. Consequently, cracking and splitting parallel the normal decline in our basal metabolic rate (BMR) and the poor circulation which results.

Young women with poor nails often have cold hands, poor circulation, or a circulation-related problem, such as anaemia. So, the first requirement to prevent splitting is a good diet and sensible supplementation.

Nutrition and your nails

In addition to eating a good diet, there are a few other specific things you can do for your fingernails – and your hair will benefit, too.

- Unflavoured gelatin provides an extra protein load that triggers a response we call 'Specific Dynamic Action' (SDA). This causes the body to produce extra heat energy, and to get rid of the heat, blood flow increases to the hands and head. This flow, along with the extra protein, helps nourish the nail bed to produce more keratin; the hair follicles do the same.

  Take about 1 oz (25 g) of unflavoured gelatin daily in water or juice to improve fingernails. You will notice results in about one month. Gelatin will also increase metabolism.

- Rather than taking gelatin, you could use a protein supplement that will also nourish the rest of your body. It should include the B-complex of vitamins to help your nails even more. Again, it will take at least a month to see results.

Always be sure that your nails are strong and you can see a nice, pinkish glow beneath them. It is a simple means of evaluating your circulation and gives some indication of your nutrition. Keep your nails healthy and you will be healthy.

Now let us look at ways you can care for your hands, feet and nails by means of massage, exercise and grooming, to keep them strong, supple and attractive.

CARING FOR YOUR HANDS

We put a heavy work load on our hands, and they are on display virtually every minute of the day, but very few of us spend much time looking after them. Few men have ever had a manicure; and though most women give themselves a manicure occasionally, it is often hurriedly done.

127

This is a pity, because hands are an integral part of our appeal and the way that they look adds to or detracts from our charm and well-groomed appearance. They are also one of the first parts of our body to show tell-tale signs of ageing. Always wear gloves when washing-up and never put your hands in detergent solution. Apply a good handcream regularly – and after every time your hands have been in water. Age spots can be prevented with good diet and supplementation (see Chapter 2), and a change of diet for the better has been known to result in existing age spots fading.

Fortunately, given a little tender loving care, neglected hands soon can look noticeably better. So resolve now to give them a few seconds' exercise and massage every day, and a careful manicure every week.

Manicure tips

Half an hour is sufficient time for a manicure.

1. Remove old polish, if necessary: use an oily polish remover.

2. Shape nails: use clippers to shorten the nails (move from right to centre, then left to centre, then finally across the top). File each nail to a smooth edge, using an emery board and tilting it slightly so that filing is confined to the underside of the free edge. File each nail from corner to centre, going from right to left, then left to right. Use two short quick strokes and one long sweeping stroke.

3. Soften cuticles: use cuticle oil to massage each nail gently, then immerse the nails in mild soapy water for about five minutes. If your hands are stained, gently brush away these marks.

4. Dry your fingernails, at the same time gently pushing back the cuticle on each nail.

5. Apply cuticle remover: wind a thin layer of cotton wool around the blunt end of an orange stick for an applicator.

6. Use the spoon end of the cuticle pusher and, with a slightly rolling motion, very gently loosen each cuticle.

7. Use pumice stone gently around each nail if necessary, and exfoliating cream or an oat-filled pouch all over hands and nails.

8. Clean under tips of nails, using a cotton-tipped orange stick.

9. Bleach under nail tips, using a cotton-tipped orange stick moistened with lemon juice or hydrogen peroxide.

10. Apply cuticle oil or cream around the sides and base of each nail and gently massage with the thumb.

11. Wash and dry your hands thoroughly.

12. Gently massage your hands and nails with hand lotion.

13. Gently buff your nails, working in one direction only, using a nail buffer.

Hand exercises

For the best results, massage and exercise the hands several times a week: more often if they feel tense and stiff.

1. Massage each finger from tip to base. Use the thumb and first finger of your other hand with a light wringing motion. Massage all your fingers and both thumbs in this way.

2. Let your hands go limp and flop them up and down several times or flutter them fast while holding them above your head.

3. Relax your hands by interlocking your fingers and pulling your hands away from each other. (Practise holding your hands in a relaxed position when they are at rest, rather than stiff and tense.)

4. Hold your index finger with the thumb and first finger of your other hand and rotate it in a circular motion. In turn, move each finger and thumb of both hands in a similar manner.

5. Use the thumb and index finger of one hand to grip the knuckle of the thumb of the other hand and move the thumb in a circle. Repeat for each finger and thumb.

6. Make both of your hands into relaxed fists and rotate both from the wrists, in a clockwise direction. Repeat in an anticlockwise direction.

7. Grasp one hand with the other, placing the thumb at the base of the palm of your hand and your fingers at the back. Press the thumb firmly on the base and commence moving it upwards towards the base of the fingers, pressing as you go. Then, massage the back of your hand from the base to the finger tips. Repeat for the other hand.

8. Press the fleshy portion between your left thumb and index finger at least five times. Repeat action for your right thumb and index finger.

9. Gently but firmly press your left thumb down towards your left wrist – DO NOT use force. Now press your thumb in the opposite direction, towards the back of your hand. Work each finger in the same way. Repeat for other hand.

10. Stretch the fingers and thumbs of both hands as wide open as you can, then close them again. Repeat 20 times.

Always end a session by shaking both hands loosely from the wrist. Then relax.

CARING FOR YOUR FEET

If you give your feet a few minutes' care daily you will stand straighter, walk better, and develop fewer facial lines – when your feet hurt, it always shows on your face.

When ever you bathe or shower, use a soft complexion brush on your toes and a regular nail brush or loofah on your soles and heels. Also, wash thoroughly between your toes with a deodorant soap or lotion.

Every time you dry your feet, ease back the cuticles around your toenails with the towel. Always dry your feet thoroughly; prolonged dampness between the toes provides a breeding ground for fungus infections. Then, massage your feet briefly with exfoliating cream or pumiceaway any flaky dead skin; this will help prevent calluses. Follow with a light dusting of anti-perspirant foot powder.

General care

To keep skin around the toenails from becoming hardened and to help ward off ingrown toenails, rub with petroleum jelly and leave it on overnight.

- When your feet are especially tired, sit on the edge of the bath and run first hand-hot water, then cold, over them. Dry them thoroughly. Follow with a cooling mist of cologne.

- Always buy stockings, tights or socks a half size larger than your shoe size so you can move your toes freely in them.

- If your feet develop any redness or swelling, especially around the big toe, check the fit of your shoes. Foot sizes (in width and length) change over the years, so at the slightest hint of rubbing, tightness or irritation, stop wearing the shoes that cause the problem. The disfiguring and painful bunion – a chronic inflamation of the big toe joint – is usually the result of wearing shoes that are too short or too pointed.

- If you have painful corns, calluses or signs of a bunion, see a chiropodist for professional treatment. A few visits can prevent real foot trouble.

Self-treatment is not advisable even for such 'minor' tasks as removing a deep-rooted corn, as you run the risk of causing a serious infection.

Foot exercises

1. Sitting comfortably in a chair with your feet off the floor, extend your toes – at the same time feeling the stretch from your ankle to your toes along the top half of your foot. Now stretch the muscles along the outside of your feet by turning your feet inwards. Then pull your toes upwards towards your legs and feel the pull along the sole. Repeat 10 times.

2. To lengthen the outside muscles, turn the toes and feet outwards. With both feet, stretch your big toe and draw big circles, first in one direction, then the other, 20 times each way.

3. Cross your legs and rotate the free, uppermost foot in a clockwise circular motion 20 times, then anticlockwise 20 times. Change legs and repeat.

4. Roll each foot back and forth on a tennis ball, 20 times for each foot.

5. Stand and rise on to your toes. Hold for count of 5. Lower your heel. Repeat 10 times.

TEETH AND GUMS

Your teeth put the sunshine in your smile and create people's first impression of you. But teeth do far more than impart good looks; they are essential to good digestion and overall good health. What's more, losing teeth can have a major ageing effect on the face. For example, it will cause wrinkles around both lips and your lips will tend to sag. Tooth loss is, however, completely preventable with a few daily habits. Then, with a little more effort, our teeth can be made to shine like the stars.

Preventing tooth decay

Cavities are caused when the natural bacteria that grow as a film, called plaque, on the surface of our teeth come in contact with the wrong foods – for example, too much sugar. Sweet, sticky confections cause the bacteria to produce acid that dissolves tooth enamel. This acid creates small openings in the enamel and a bacterial infection starts inside the tooth. This infection, a cavity, can only be corrected by drilling out the decay, eliminating the bacteria, and restoring the tooth's surface with a filling. Once a cavity has been filled, the tooth is never the same; so, prevention is the best cure. Cavities are prevented by following a few simple rules.

Dental hygiene: prevent cavities

- Brush 3 minutes with a toothpaste after each meal. Fluoride toothpaste helps build stronger tooth enamel.

- Floss after each meal and after brushing to remove any food particles that lodge between the teeth. It is important that the floss go below the gum line to get any food particles out.

- Rinse your mouth by swishing warm water or a hygienic antibacterial rinse between the teeth. This reduces plaque build-up.

- Some toothpastes contain sanguinerin, a herb, or special enzymes which help reduce plaque. When using such dentifrice, don't rinse after brushing.

- Have a dental check-up every year, along with a thorough cleaning by a dental hygienist.

Diet

- Don't eat sugary foods and confectionary. The stickier they are, the worse.

- Finish every meal with fruit, such as an apple: never eat dried fruit after or between meals, because it sticks to the teeth and causes dental caries. Cheese is an excellent after-dinner accompaniment with dessert; it contains calcium which helps the teeth stay strong, and encourages the production of saliva which cleans the teeth and helps prevent cavities.

- After eating, rinse your mouth with water, swishing and forcing it between the teeth; an antibacterial mouthwash is better than water.

Healthy gums

Strong, healthy gums are the result of good diet and good nutrition. Foods that impact in between the gum and tooth accelerate periodontal disease (periodontal means surrounding the teeth). Periodontal disease develops when bacteria become established between the tooth and gum. Toxins produced by the bacteria can destroy the connective tissue between the gum, tooth, and bone, which causes tooth loss. Similar to cavities, the best cure for periodontal disease is prevention.

Gum problems usually begin with gingivitis which is characterised by mild bleeding of the gums after flossing, brushing, or eating hard food, such as crackers. Gingivitis is aggravated by acidic, sweet foods, such as carbonated beverages and confectionary. Foods that impact around the gum line can become hardened into a plaster-like substance called tartar. This tartar allows bacteria to grow, causing a periodontal infection between the tooth and gum. Tartar is removed by regular flossing and brushing.

Research has proven that gingivitis is often an indication that you require more vitamin C than average people. Clinical studies show that some people who have gingivitis require as much as 500 mg of vitamin C daily to maintain healthy gums and stop the gingivitis. If your gums have a tendency to bleed, taking 500 mg of vitamin C in addition to the diet we recommend is good health insurance.

Promote healthy gums

- Eat soft, sugary foods, such as cakes and breads that tend to impact around the base of the teeth, in moderation. Try to brush and rinse your mouth immediately after eating these types of foods.

- Use a fluoride toothpaste.

- When brushing, gently stroke down from the top and up from the bottom, massaging the gums. This motion helps pull food particles from between the gums and teeth.

- Don't smoke; it increases the risk of periodontal disease.

- Floss after each meal, taking care to use a section of clean, waxed thread for the base of each tooth. Look in the mirror to learn how to go below the gum line with dental floss.

- Drink sweet beverages sparingly; especially carbonated beverages.

- If you have gingivitis, take extra vitamin C.

- Have an annual dental check-up which should include a thorough cleaning.

Can teeth be brighter?

You can keep your teeth healthy and white with good hygiene, but your dentist can help as well. Sometimes teeth become dull and almost yellowish over the years as a result of food staining. Smoking can have the same effect. Your dentist can eliminate this stain with a mild bleaching and restore a youthful whiteness to your teeth. At your next dental examination, ask about this brightening procedure.

Dare to smile

As we have already stated – and research proves this – tooth decay is no accident but is closely related to total body condition. For many, the advice given in this chapter may come too late to make any difference. Not all is lost, however, and you can still have a great smile; false teeth today are more natural looking than they were in the past. In addition, progress has been made in corrective and cosmetic dentistry, and dentists themselves are becoming more skilled in the art of capping, crowning, implanting, sealing, cosmetically contouring, and bleaching or covering dull and yellowish stains with porcelain or plastic coveralls.

Consult your dentist or a specialist cosmetic dentist for further advice on the many treatments available and their cost. Corrective dentistry will not only help to give you a great youthful looking smile, but will increase your self confidence.

· CHAPTER ELEVEN ·

Good Posture and You

In the past, the Chinese bound the feet of their daughters so they would have baby-like feet for life, because it was thought the girls would make faithful wives if they could not run. Even as adults, these women had to be carried around like infants.

Binding feet is just one example of how people changed bodily growth. In our western society, the way you carry yourself – your posture – influences the most important organ of all, your brain. It also has an effect on the function of your internal organs and directly influences your spine, which affects the anatomy of your entire skeleton. This influences the size, location and space of your internal organs, including your kidneys, liver and digestive system. Posture can change your height by inches.

Thus, your posture affects your physical ability, appearance, health and outlook on the world around you.

Posture power and your spine

Your spine or backbone is arranged on your hips and supported by your legs; it supports your ribcage, shoulders, and head. But the spine is not a single bone. It consists of 19 small, plate-like bones called vertebrae, separated from each other by discs of a tough, slippery, hard, rubber-like tissue called cartilage. We get two major advantages from this structure: flexibility and shock absorption.

Our spine is flexible; you can demonstrate that to yourself by first standing straight then hunching over. Our spine is a shock absorber because each bone and disc can compress and expand slightly. For example, you are a little taller in the morning because you have had no weight on your spine all night; in contrast, in the evening it has been supporting your head, shoulders and any extra weight you have carried during the day. You can prove this by measuring yourself first thing in the morning, and then again in the evening.

Running from our brain down the centre of the spine is the spinal cord, the most important nerve in our body. Think of it as a trunk nerve-line from the brain. Running off between each vertebra are nerves that go to specific parts of the body. The spinal cord handles many functions directly; it does not need your brain.

For example, when you touch your finger to a flame – you will pull it back instantly. The nerve impulse that detected the heat travelled to your spinal cord, which sent instructions to pull back all in an instant. More complex examples range from walking to kidney function and letting you know when your bladder is full.

Poor posture can put uneven pressure on a disc, causing the disc to weaken on one side and pinch a nerve. This prevents part of your body from having correct feeling and function, and the uneven disc creates intense back-pain, because the spinal cord is being compressed.

Chiropractic is dedicated to the influence of the spine and posture on our body. Practitioners teach that many malfunctions of the body are the result of poor nerve-function at the spine; in other words, the location of the discs and vertebrae. The chiropractor manipulates each vertebra and disc into its correct position, thus eliminating many functional problems which are usually the result of poor posture.

Nourish your spine Your spinal column is a shock absorber. For example, you jump, step, run, go up and down stairs, and carry things that shock your spine, but your head is not bounced and shocked by all this movement. It is the spine that absorbs these shocks because we have hard rubber-like discs between each vertebra and each vertebra is soft and spongy compared to other bones, like the leg or arm. So the spine absorbs shock like firm rubber and not like a rigid rod. However, if you do not nourish your spine correctly, the bones become too porous and each vertebra will be squashed by your body weight. Therefore, good posture and good nutrition are essential to a healthy spine.

The Longevity Diet provides good nutrition for the spine. However, as we age, we need increasing amounts of calcium. As we tend to neglect dairy products (not many adults drink their allotment of milk every day) we may need to take calcium supplements if we want to keep our bones strong. But is does not end there.

Osteoporosis

As women age, the balance of their hormones changes. This balance goes through an abrupt change during menopause, a ten-year period, usually beginning at age 45 to 50. During menopause, calcium content in the bones declines more rapidly because of the normal hormonal changes, and the spine is one of the first bones to lose its calcium. All experts agree that women over 45 need 1,000 mg of calcium daily and many experts argue that they need 1,500 mg. Once the menstrual cycle stops, some experts believe women should take hormones plus 1,000 mg of calcium; or without hormones, 2,000 mg of calcium daily, to maintain good bone-density throughout the body.

Research has shown that a small amount of the hormone oestrogen, along with 1,500 mg of calcium, works wonders. A group of post-menopausal women on this regimen had no decline in bone density compared to women who took either the calcium or the oestrogen alone.

Osteoporosis is not a disease of ageing as many people think. It is the result of marginal calcium-deficiency, usually beginning as a teenager, that shows up after menopause. Prevention is the best cure.

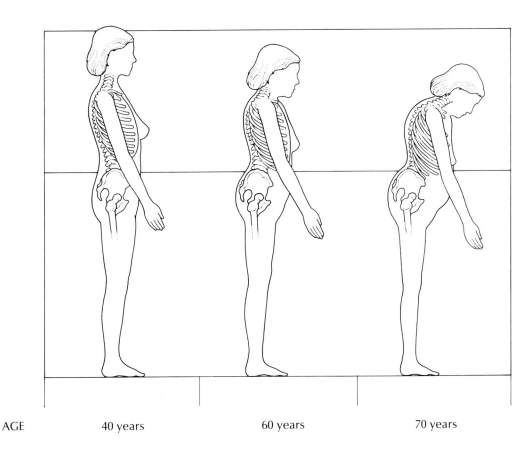

| AGE | 40 years | 60 years | 70 years |

The diagram on page 137 illustrates how we shrink with age. It is a schematic side-view of a woman who neglects her nutritional needs and allows her vertebrae to squash down. It shows more slowly in men because they start with a higher bone-density and do not have the dramatic hormonal changes women experience.

Why bones lose density As people age, their bones adapt to a more sedentary, less active lifestyle and become less dense (dense means weight per unit of volume). As bones lose density they become full of holes where the calcium has leached out. Under a microscope, they look like Swiss cheese or a sponge. They become more brittle. Brittle bones are dangerous because they don't break like a stick but shatter like glass and are very hard to mend.

In the ideal person, bone density increases up to about the age of 20 or 25, remains fixed until around age 50 and then usually begins to decline. However, bones do not have to decline; both men and women can have strong bones past the age of 125, if they eat a good diet and exercise regularly.

In the average person, bone density increases to about age 15 or 20, remains constant to age 35 or 40 and then begins a slow decline, which increases more for women at age 40 or 45 due to the menopause (see page 137). Bone density continues to go down after that.

The decline is the outcome of three forces at work: not enough calcium and exercise and, for most of us, too much meat. We never outgrow our need for calcium and exercise. Lack of exercise will cause a decline in bone density even if you do drink enough milk. If you don't use bones, you lose bones! Also, as our protein from meat increases, we seem to need more calcium. The reasons for this are unclear; but we know that people who don't eat as much meat as we do get along on less calcium. Oriental women, who are mostly vegetarian, are excellent examples; they do perfectly well on 200–300 mg of calcium daily.

So, exercise with the right diet will help restore bone density. As the bones improve, they add to LBM and help adjust the body fat downwards. The reward is better health into the golden years.

Jean's story Jean, age 42, asked to have lunch with me in Vancouver, Canada, where she heard me speak. She was short, hunched over, had a 'pot' belly and seemed in pain, and explained that she had lost six inches (15 cm) in height due to crushed vertebrae. Also, her bone-density, as determined by x-ray, was 40% of normal. Her doctor had advised her to take calcium supplements.

I asked if she had ever had surgery, and she replied that she had undergone a complete hysterectomy and had her ovaries removed eight years ago.

I asked: 'Were you put on hormones?'

She said that she was, but stopped taking them six years ago because someone told her she could make up for them by taking other vitamins.

I explained that, without the hormones, her body would not add new calcium to her bones. In effect, she had been removing calcium from her bones for six years; it was as if she had been getting no dietary calcium. We immediately called her doctor to explain what she had done, so he could put her back on the hormones and the calcium. Two years later, Jean's bone-density had improved steadily. However, she will never get her height or posture back. She will have strong, but squashed-out vertebrae.

Once a vertebra has become compressed from poor density combined with poor posture, it can not be reversed. You can restore the bone density to what it should have been, but its shape has been changed for good. Do not let it happen to you.

Low back pain   Declining bone-density and poor posture usually sound a preliminary warning signal: low-back pain – an undefined ache at the base of your spine where it meets the hips. Your doctor may arrange for you to have x-rays which, in this case, usually show nothing, and you may then be told the back pain is part of ageing. To ageing, I say hogwash!

Dr. Tony Albanese, a research scientist at the Burke Rehabilitation Center in America, took women volunteers, with low back pain that could not be traced to any specific problems, and measured their bone density; it was about 65% of what it should have been. He started them on a regimen of calcium supplements, exercise and good posture; in menopausal women, oestrogen was also included. The bone density of these women increased. When it reached about 90% of what it should have been, the back pain disappeared.

When the bone density of these women reached normal for their ages, Dr. Albanese switched the calcium or calcium and oestrogen with a placebo and kept the women on the regimen. When their bone density dropped below 90% of normal again, the back pain usually returned. His studies on bone improvement have included women from age 35–82. He proved you are never too young or too old to improve your condition.

The problem with nutrition is that it takes time, the rewards come slowly and often aren't even noticed. It takes eight to twelve months for the bone density to increase by 10% on average. It is faster for some people and slower for others.

Room to work

Poor posture affects all your organs. If they could speak, they would probably say one thing in unison: 'give me room to do my job'. The human body is packed with organs and tissue. Each organ has alloted space and needs good nutrition to do its job.

A demonstration   Stand back against an empty wall with your feet, shoulders, arms, buttocks and head touching it. Breathe deeply and fill your lungs to capacity, then exhale. Now hunch way over and breathe deeply again. Notice the difference? When you are hunched over, the muscles that pull your lungs open can not work effectively; you can not breathe as deeply. Your body, including your brain, does not get as much oxygen as when you stand straight. Just by changing the way you stand, you have first increased, then reduced your lung capacity. If you were hunched over all the time, you would always breathe at 40% less capacity. So, your posture should be erect, shoulders back, legs straight and head held high.

Two points are essential: posture influences how your internal organs work; if you have an incorrect posture long enough, there is no going back to what you were or could have been. However, bones grow and change all through life, so posture, diet and exercise can restore bone strength in people at any age; even over the age of 80. Make posture power work for you; not against you.

Competitive male cyclists illustrate how posture affects function. By bending over the handle bars, they keep wind resistance to a minimum, but they also cramp their pelvis and abdomen. This presses their prostate gland against the blood vessels and nerves going to the penis. The result of prolonged cycling is the inability to achieve an erection and to perform sexually. The effect wears off in 10–12 hours, but it shows how posture can cause problems.

You can demonstrate effects on other organs in your own body. Slumping way over and trying to take a deep breath like you did earlier is a simple example.

Posture exercises

Maintaining strong back muscles and limbering your vertebrae will pay big dividends. You will find it easy to hold a good posture, be less likely to have back pain and be able to sit erect much longer. The exercises are simple, but they strengthen the important muscles.

- Lie flat on your stomach on a firm surface. Put your hands behind your back and clasp them together. Holding your legs stiff, raise your chest and legs off the floor at the same time, as high as you can. Hold for five seconds then slowly return to the starting position. Start by doing this once in the morning and again in the evening. Work up to five, twice daily; 10 is better. This is the easiest way to stretch, tone and strengthen the back.

- This exercise is even easier. Stand facing into a corner of a room about 1 ft (30 cm) out from the corner. Holding your arms shoulder high, bend your elbows and place your palms against each wall with fingertips touching. When you are standing correctly, you will be looking at each hand which will be about 8 in (20 cm) from the corner and about as high as your neck.

  Now simply push with both hands equally, as if to push the walls away. Push for the count of five, relax and then do it again. Repeat five times in the morning and again in the evening.

  This exercise will strengthen the muscles and tendons of the shoulders. It has very little visible effect, because it is strictly a preventive exercise. It will prevent you from slouching as you get older. You will know it has been worth it at age 60, when your posture is still erect and some of your contemporaries are slouching.

Walking tall

Posture is a habit like everything else. Gravity tries to pull us down so it takes effort to stand tall and straight. Youth in body and mind, that's what a good posture reflects, and it certainly makes you look and feel younger. So it is well worth making a conscientious effort to cultivate an upright posture. Every time you find your shoulders and your chest sagging forward and your abdomen sagging downwards, mentally as well as physically correct your stance and your sagging thoughts.

When you walk into a room, the way you carry yourself, your posture, will tell the people around you a great deal about your confidence or lack of it. Slumping, slouching or shuffling will give out signals that you are a weak or submissive person. If, on the other hand, you have good posture and stance, you will project an image of someone who is confident and comfortable in his or her situation.

The ideal posture is neither too stiff, nor too relaxed or slouched. So lower your shoulders, straighten your back, hold your head a little higher and control your abdominal muscles.

If you have naturally rounded shoulders or are stooped, you still need to work towards the best posture possible. Do the posture exercises described earlier and walk as erect as possible. It will pay the same dividends for you.

Our posture, dress and daily habits all go together. If you must carry a heavy briefcase or some other equipment regularly, alternate your arms and be sure to stand tall. If possible, support the weight with a trolley or some other device. If you climb in and out of the cab of a delivery van, alternate the way you step up and down. The reasons are clear: your body adjusts to these routines. Before long, one arm is slightly longer, your shoulders become stronger, etc. Then, your backbone will be stressed on one side more than the other, or a muscle will enlarge over another, and you will be permanently changed.

High-heeled shoes make you look great and stand tall, but do so at a price. They cause muscles to shrink, put excessive pressure on the ball of your foot and at the base of your spine. Does this mean you shouldn't keep up with fashion? Of course not. However, it means you should alternate with low-heeled shoes or only use high heels when you'll be doing more sitting than walking.

Varicose veins

Everyone wants to avoid varicose veins. These veins occur when blood pools in our legs as a result of poor circulation. So, sitting correctly can help reduce the risk of getting them. A few rules will help:

- Sit with feet on the floor so the circulation is not cut off.

- Don't cross your legs for extended periods of time. If you must cross them, alternate every 15 minutes.

- Get up and walk a little every hour. This is especially important if your job requires sitting.

- Do not strain when having a bowel movement and do not sit for long periods on the toilet.

- Make sure you get enough fibre so you have an easy bowel movement once in 24 to 36 hours.

- Be sure to exercise your legs by walking, jogging or swimming.

Line design: the illusion of good posture

Used carefully, line design can create the illusion of balance and good posture or, used badly, emphasise imbalance and an ageing stance. When we refer to line we are referring to the outline of a garment and the style lines within this that seem to divide the garment up. A line will lead the eye and can be used to create optical illusions.

Vertical lines   These can be used to draw attention away from bad posture. When vertical lines are used on a dress or outfit less attention is focused on the actual outline of the figure, as the eye is kept busy travelling up and down the vertical lines.

Horizontal lines   A poor posture, an ageing stance, rounded shoulders and an overweight figure can be visibly transformed with the use of shoulder pads. By making the shoulders appear to be the broadest part of your body, you are creating a horizontal line of width which visually balances the rest of your body and allows your clothes to hang freely from the shoulders. Shoulder pads can give a flatter look to a back that has started to hunch, and a straighter look to stooped or rounded shoulders. As a result the body's outline will look more streamlined and youthful. The wearing of shoulder pads is also a constant reminder to you to live up to your image and cultivate an upright posture.

CHAPTER TWELVE

The Impact of Colour

The colours you wear play a very important role in the overall impression you give out: young or old, powerful, approachable, playful, energetic or lethargic, appropriate or inappropriate, taller or smaller. Wearing your positive colours will enhance your looks: your complexion will look smoother; lines, wrinkles and blemishes will seem less apparent. Even a man's 'five o'clock shadow' will be less noticeable. The reason for this is that your skin will not be picking up and reflecting negative colours which do not relate to your natural colouring. If you complement your own positive colour characteristics when choosing clothing, you will create a harmonious, pleasing and flattering effect.

You have already determined your colouring in Chapter 7. Now let's learn how to use this knowledge to choose the most flattering colours to wear.

Choosing the most flattering colours

What are your first and second colour characteristics? Use the first as a basic around which to build your wardrobe. Your second is best used to add more colour to your look and wardrobe. The colour fans between pages 96 and 97 show you your best colours to wear.

Dark: you will always look best with a dark colour included in your look.

Dark/bright: you wear dark/bright and dark/light colour combinations which give strong colour contrasts best. Avoid a blended look or two dark colours together without adding a bright or light accent.

Dark/muted: wear dark/muted and dark/bright colour combinations with dark to medium or soft contrast. Avoid bright and light colours together without adding a dark accent.

All darks: avoid two light-colour combinations, without a dark or bright accent.

Light: you look best with some light colours in your look.

Light/bright: wear light and bright colours with light to medium contrast. Avoid blended looks.

Light/muted: wear light muted combinations with light to medium soft contrast. Avoid strong contrast.

Bright: bring some brightness into your overall look.

Bright/dark: wear bright/dark and light colours, and strong contrast best.

Bright/light: wear bright/light combinations with bright and light contrast.

All brights: avoid blended looks or two dark colours together.

Muted: a slightly heavy, toned-down look to your colours is best. Wear soft contrast and blended looks.

Muted/dark: wear two medium or medium and dark tones together, or in combination. Wear medium contrast and blended looks.

Muted/light: wear muted/light combinations with medium to light contrast. Avoid two dark colour combinations.

All muted: avoid strong contrast.

Warm: some warmth should be added to your look.

Warm/dark: wear warm combinations with medium to dark contrast and blended looks; avoid strong contrast.

Warm/light: wear warm and light combinations with medium to light contrast.

All warms: avoid strong cool undertones.

Cool: wear blue undertone or slightly toned down colour effects.

Cool/dark: wear cool-dark combinations with medium to dark contrast.

Cool/light: wear cool-light combinations with medium to light contrast.

All cools: avoid strong warm undertones.

What about the clothes in your wardrobe which don't fit into your characteristics? No problem; just team them with ties, blouses, scarves and jewellery which fit into your first and second characteristics.

For instance take a light/bright person who has to wear a dark navy suit. On its own this would take them over and grab all the attention, making dark shadows reflect on the skin so it looks older and less attractive. They could make a navy suit look in harmony with their natural colouring in the following ways:

Light/bright men By wearing a light shirt and a bright, medium intensity tie to bridge the big gap between the dark suit and the light shirt, bringing them closer together and reducing the contrast. At the same time, some lightness and brightness have been introduced.

Light/bright women Do the same with a light blouse and bright jewellery, scarves and pocket handkerchiefs.

Colours worn together can increase or decrease one another's colour characteristic and create a different look or mood, for instance:

- Wearing white with a clear, bright colour such as red, makes the red look lighter and brighter.

- Put black with the red and it looks darker and heavier.

- Ivory or beiges make it look softer.

- Put blue red with it and it will take on a warm look.

- An orange red next to it, will make it look slightly blue-red.

A simple colour test

As the years go by we lose some of the pigment in our skin, hair and eyes, lessening our body's level of contrast. For this reason, we may find we have to soften some of our looks.

Train your eyes to tell you when a colour is right for you. For example, to see if you have grown out of the 'white' white and into the 'softer' white or clear ivory, drape a whiter than white garment over one shoulder and a soft white or ivory over the other. Looking into a mirror, close your eyes for a second and then open them. Whichever colour is demanding attention is *not* your best shade of colour. This colour is wearing you, instead of vice versa. The colour which allows you to look at your face and eyes is best, because it doesn't take you over. This test works on all shades and intensities, and practice makes perfect.

Whenever you are trying on new clothes and are undecided about a particular colour, look into the mirror and if the colour of the garment gives the impression of being closer to the mirror than you are, then the colour is wearing you. Try a different colour or different shade of the same colour, or look for ways of softening the overpowering effect.

Neutrals

Bright colours cannot only date quickly, but can call too much attention to what you are wearing and overpower your personality. You may also tire of them quickly.

Neutrals, on the other hand, do not date but are thought of as 'classics', and they don't overwhelm the wearer. Because of this they are a useful addition to your wardrobe.

Broadly speaking, a neutral is any colour which has black, white or grey added to it to such an extent that it has changed its description. For example; blue with enough black added becomes navy blue. Yellow with enough black added will become dark green. Black and white themselves are not colours in the true sense, in that they have no 'hue'. For our purposes we class them as 'basic neutrals.'

'Coloured neutrals' are three or more colours mixed together, turning them into a nondescript colour which we would call beige, grey or brown depending on how much white or black was added.

Building a wardrobe around neutrals, especially for large items of clothing such as coats, jackets, suits etc., will stretch your wardrobe as they mix and match well, and will make it last longer as neutrals never go out of fashion.

Neutrals on their own can look drab, boring and ageing, and so are usually best when some colour is added to the outfit, particularly for people who have 'Bright' as their first or second colour characteristic. However, mixing different intensities of neutrals to create interest can look stunning on anyone who has dark or muted as their first or second colour characteristic.

The thing to remember as you mature is to choose your neutrals, as with all colours, with care. Never let them take you over, which would be very ageing and emphasise every line on your face, in addition to drawing attention to your outline (which may or may not be desirable).

- Wearing the two extremes of black and white together will create a strong sharp contrast which gives an assertive look.

- The softest neutrals are shades of ivory, beige, tan and brown. When these are worn together they give a softer, less assertive look than the above. They can also be used to soften the above look: for example, shades of brown and beige that suit you worn with black and white gives a very sophisticated look which could take you anywhere.

- Some neutrals are created by mixing black with a colour until it is almost but not quite black itself; for example, mahogany, pine green and royal purple. In almost every case such neutrals are more gentle on the skin than black.

- Similarly, colours which are mixed with white until they almost become white, such as ivorys and beiges, are generally easier to wear than pure white.

Primary and basic colours

The three primary colours are bright in character. They are true red, blue and yellow.

- True primary colours are best worn by those whose first characteristic is bright. However, as you mature you may need to adjust what you wear with them, or move to a slightly less bright shade of red, blue or yellow the next time you make a purchase.

- Adding a white blouse or shirt to an outfit in bright red, blue or yellow would give a very lively, bright colour combination. Alternatively adding an off-white, ivory, beige or light grey blouse or shirt would give an active young combination which is less attention grabbing and easier to wear.

- The basic colours of green, violet and turquoise are youthful and bright in character, but are less bright than the primaries and easier to wear by most people. Romantic colours such as peach, pink, aqua and pale blue are lighter and softer and have a gentle effect on the skin.

- A white, or soft white, shirt or blouse will always make a dark suit look crisp and assertive.

- A light pastel or ivory coloured shirt or blouse will soften the dark suit as well as any facial lines which have started to appear.

- A blouse, shirt or tie worn with a dark suit will look different when worn with a medium-intensity suit.

- A bright or medium-intensity blouse, shirt or tie will attract more attention to the wearer.

Colour co-ordination for women

Women have a much wider choice of colours for clothes than men do (although manufacturers are now trying to encourage men to wear brighter colours). This is one reason why women make more mistakes; many will admit that they have a wardrobe full of clothes and nothing to wear.

Women buy in a rush or on impulse more often than men do. They see a colour they like and often buy it, with insufficient thought as to what message the colour will convey, whether it does anything for them, or whether it combines well with the rest of their wardrobe, because colour response is emotional as well as physical. Bear this in mind when you next shop for clothes and try to stick to the following guidelines:

When considering a colour, ask yourself:

- What does this colour do for me?

- What effect do I want to create, and what colours will best convey this effect?

- What effect do I want the colours I am wearing to have on *me*?

- Are these colours appropriate for my intended audience?

- Are these colours appropriate for the occasion?

- Could I improve on my look?

- Does it bring my looks to life, or make me look grey and washed out?

Mixing and matching colour: what goes with what

Jacket and skirts	Blouse	Handkerchief, Scarf, Belt and Jewellery
Light	Dark	Medium or patterned
Dark	Light	Medium
Medium	Light	Medium
Plain	Patterned	Plain
Patterned	Plain/medium	Plain/light or dark

Creating different looks with colour

Use a scarf, belt or jewellery to change the overall appearance of an outfit, say from day into evening wear. An accessory colour can lift, quieten or co-ordinate a whole look. When wearing different coloured separates, always bring them together in some way. For example, a colour worn on the lower half of the body should always be repeated by some means on the upper half. This could be by way of a blouse, jacket, scarf, handkerchief, jewellery or even a small amount of the colour in the patterned fabric or piping.

Colour co-ordination for men

Now that men have more colour choices, dressing well is becoming a little trickier – but if you keep these guidelines in mind you will always look right:

- Your tie should be a different shade or contrasting colour to your suit and shirt.

- When wearing separates, such as a navy blazer and grey trousers, repeat the grey in the pattern of your tie, or the stripe of your shirt, to co-ordinate your look.

- When mixing two patterns, never have them the same size or intensity of colour.

In the chart below there is a contrast in the shade between the suit, tie and shirt. Let your personal colour values be your guide to the amount of contrast you should aim for.

Mixing and matching colour

Suit	Shirt	Tie, Handkerchief, Scarf
Dark	Light	Medium
Medium	Light	Dark
Light	Dark	Medium

Classics are so called because their cut and style make them dateless. They feel right for most occasions. If in doubt, wear a classic. The basic style doesn't change with the dictates of the fashion industry. For example, a 'classic' man's suit, either single- or double-breasted (whichever is best for your height), in a good quality fabric with straight-cut hips, classic lapels and single vent, will look good for many years.

CHAPTER THIRTEEN

What You Think, You Are

If you have followed the advice in each chapter of this book, reading, understanding, and carrying out each test and making the necessary adjustments to your thinking and lifestyle, you will already be looking and starting to feel excited and positive about yourself, your self-image and your potential. If, on the other hand, you are having some difficulty in following or re-programming yourself, it's because you haven't yet fully accepted or cannot believe that your desire to look and feel younger, fitter and healthier *can* be achieved. But we promise you: IT CAN.

CONTRASTS IN SUCCESS

We always find someone to credit with our success or failure. One person's reason for success can be another person's reason for failure. It depends upon how we visualise ourselves and what we visualise for ourselves. A vignette of two boys illustrates the need for the right outlook.

Identical twin boys were born to a couple whom, experts agreed, should never have lived together, let alone had children. The boys' father, an unskilled worker with no obvious ambition, never held a steady job. He drank heavily, lived from day to day and had no goals. The mother did menial tasks intermittently when she could get work. Both parents drank excessively and often lived on welfare. Both boys were raised as much by neighbours and each other, as by their parents. By the age of 10, they were almost left to raise themselves.

Survival was the word that described their home life. Their parents fought so violently at times that police were called to stop the argument; sometimes they had to sleep off their alcoholic condition at the police station. Both parents regularly beat the children and used words like 'damn kids' or 'no-good kids'. The boys' home life wasn't the foundation of a good outlook.

By the age of 35, the twin boys were a contrast in success. Tom was an unskilled worker and drank heavily, like his parents. He didn't hold jobs very long, fought with his wife and the local police knew him quite well. Tom and his wife lived in the same squalid environment where they had grown up. They were well-known to the welfare authorities and learned to take advantage of everything the government would provide.

Jim was the complete opposite. He had worked hard at menial part-time jobs, while going to school at night and at week-ends. He saved what little money he could and, when he finished school, started a small business. By the time he was 35, Jim's small company was growing; and he was becoming a wealthy man. His family life was also rewarding. He and his lovely wife worked together to raise their two small children in a harmonious atmosphere. Their modest home was neat, clean and expressed pride of ownership. They were a close, happy family, enjoyed life and were serious about their future.

A social worker doing a study about identical twins interviewed both brothers. She asked them the same questions, so as not to bias the study. Curiously, she got exactly the same answer to one pertinent question: 'Why did you become what you are today?' The answer was: 'What else could I do growing up in that place?'

Each man had exactly the same lack of opportunity and each one had a vision of himself. Tom saw himself as nothing. Jim saw himself as anything he wanted to become; he had no place to go but up. The only difference between the brothers was how they got from where they were to where they visualised themselves. For Tom, it was easy – do nothing. For Jim, it required commitment to an objective. Tom said to himself: 'This is what life is like.' Jim said to himself: 'I can always do better than this.'

The power of visualisation

A sculptress once explained how she could take a block of stone and make a beautiful statue. She said: 'The statue is already there; all I do is chip away the extra stone and smooth and polish what is left.' When pressed a little further, she explained more fully: 'Before I visualise the figure in the statue, I get to know the stone. Stone has a complex texture shaped over millions of years by the elements. Once I understand the character of the stone, the figure inside is clear and can be unlocked and live forever in harmony with the elements that created the stone.'

We can take a lesson from the sculptress and the twin boys. Forces that we don't control start to shape and build the texture of our character, before we are even aware of ourselves. These forces include heredity, our home life, the environment in which we grow – everything around us. They form the fabric that will emerge as our character.

We constantly call on all this texture to visualise our life and shape our future. As time passes, more and more of the stone of life is chipped away and parts of our statue get finished. So long as we are alive, there is always time to be better and increase the abundance of our life. The better we live in harmony with the world around us, the smoother our texture becomes.

Nothing can be accomplished without a vision. Let the vision of your future become your objective, just like Tom and Jim did; but don't sell yourself short. Only two differences separate success from failure: vision and perseverance.

Education doesn't create success, nor does physical beauty; parents can't make you succeed either. They can all help, but only you can create success. Success means visualising a general goal and reshaping it as you get closer, until you achieve it.

Ask yourself a simple, but clear question: 'What is success for me?' Recognise that the answer will change, probably annually when you are young and less frequently as you mature. Notice I said 'mature', not age. You can be mature at age 20, but not old until 80; or old and mature at age 20. I know people over 90 who still talk about the future. It gets back to success and goals.

Goal setting

Goals should be realistic but require that you stretch your capability. They should take into account your resources, but more importantly, your potential. Focus on the fundamentals:

- Love: We need to love and be loved. People who experience a loving relationship live better and longer. One objective should focus on building a lasting relationship based on love and respect. For most people, this is marriage and the family, but it can be – or include – other relationships.

- Health objectives: Never compromise on what you can become. Be as healthy as you can be, no matter what your physical qualities.

- Respect: Success with people and in commerce usually depends on just one word: respect. It starts with yourself and applies to everyone you meet.

- Career objectives: Not money! Career objectives should focus on achievements and should include milestones to measure progress.

Other goals depend on what is important in your life. If you have small children, set some goals about helping them achieve their potential in terms of good health, friends, love, respect and setting the right ideals for a bright future.

Dare to take chances

Everything about life is a series of risks from the instant of conception to the hour of death. Often the only thing that separates success from failure is the willingness to dare. It can be summarised in the following poem:

TO DARE

To laugh is to risk appearing the fool
To weep is to risk appearing sentimental
To reach for another is to risk involvement
To expose your ideas, your dreams before a crowd is
to risk their loss
To love is to risk not being loved in return
To live is to risk dying
To believe is to risk failure

Risks must be taken, because the greatest hazard in life is to risk nothing. People who don't risk avoid suffering and sorrow, but they can not learn, feel, change, grow, love and live. Chained by their attitudes, they are slaves; they have forfeited their freedom. Only a person who risks is free.

Basic good habits

Bad habits bring instant rewards; good habits can take a long time for their pay out. A smoker is instantly gratified with a mild 'high', but the non-smoker might never know that his health is superior. But sooner or later, the good habits of a clean lifestyle do pay rewards.

Basic good habits are simple:

- Diet

- Lifestyle

- Integrity

- Loving yourself and others

- Respecting yourself and others
- Caring relationships

Strive

If you don't use it you lose it. This summarises every thing about life from your mental capacity to your athletic ability.

Success is what you do when no one is looking. Sound strange? It is not. Successful people work hard when they are alone and no one is looking. It is why the concert pianist practises after the concert is over, the writer is up working at 5:00 a.m. or the successful athlete goes alone to a quiet field and hones his skill. These people learn to grade themselves. Their teachers and coaches are guides to help them discover the limits of their capability, but it is their inner drive that makes them work when no one is looking, and thus they build the capacity for success.

Index

SPECIAL READER
£10 DISCOUNT OFFER

Your very own Personalised Health and Image Profile in a leather look organiser for quick and easy reference. Your organiser will include: a specially designed eating programme, fine tuned to best suit your figure image and lifestyle; fabric samples of your best colours and how to co-ordinate them successfully; a wardrobe planner designed around your figure image and lifestyle. What you learn will help you look better, feel better and live longer. Can you afford not to accept this offer?

BODY SHAPE: Heart ☐ Curved/Hourglass ☐ Ellipse ☐ Pear ☐ Straight ☐ Anglular ☐

FACE SHAPE: Oval ☐ Oblong ☐ Straight ☐ Pear ☐ Round ☐ Rectangular ☐ Heart ☐ Diamond ☐

DO YOUR WEAR GLASSES: yes ☐ no ☐

FIRST COLOUR CHARACTERISTIC: Light ☐ Bright ☐ Dark ☐ Muted ☐ Warm ☐ Cool ☐

SECOND COLOUR CHARACTERISTIC: Light ☐ Bright ☐ Dark ☐ Muted ☐ Warm ☐ Cool ☐

WHERE DO YOU PUT WEIGHT ON FIRST AND LOSE IT LAST:

Waist and above ☐ Hips and Things ☐ Waist and stomach ☐

ARE YOUR WRISTS: Slim ☐ Average ☐ Broad ☐

ARE YOUR ANKLES: Slim ☐ Average ☐ Broad ☐

HEIGHT _____ WEIGHT _____ OCCUPATION _____

HOBBIES _____

I enclose a cheque for £ _____ or debit my credit card as follows: Access/Master ☐   Visa ☐

Card Number ☐☐☐☐☐☐☐☐☐☐☐☐☐☐☐☐   Expiry date _____

Signature for credit card transactions _____

Name _____ Phone No. _____

Address _____

_____

Please mail to: Colour and Style File Ltd
                Freepost 29
                London W1E 3UZ

Do not affix postage stamps if posted in Great Britain, Channel Islands or Northern Ireland.

The Personal Organiser is normally £27.95. Special Reader Discount Price £17.95 (plus £1.00 for UK post and packing or £4 for overseas)
(If you do not wish to remove this page, please copy your answers onto a seperate sheet of paper).

LEARN HOW TO LOOK 10 YEARS YOUNGER
AND FEEL 10 YEARS BETTER

Two days of Personal Discovery. Join us on one of our Health and Image Weekends with professional advice on:

> Blood Pressure
> Body Fat
> Stress
> Personal Exercise Programme

Learn how to eat to improve your:

> Health, Energy and Figure Image

Dress for your lifestyle:

> Colour, Style, Wardrobe Planning

Leave the weekend having learnt about yourself with a permanent record contained in a Personal Organiser which contains your very own Personalised Health, Colour and Image Profile. This information will be valuable for the rest of your life.

ONE DAY OF DISCOVERY

Join us for a Top to Toe Colour and Style assessment. Our colour and style consultancy also includes Wardrobe Planning around your lifestyle. You leave with all your details recorded in a personal organiser.

Please rush me details of your Health and Image Weekends on how to Look and Feel Better and your One Day of Discovery.

Name _____ Phone No. _____

Address _____

_____

Please mail to: Colour and Style File Ltd
                  Freepost 29
                  London W1E 3UZ